ONLINE LEARNING AND COURSE DESIGN

2 books in 1: The comprehensive quick start guide to bring your virtual digital classroom to the next level with ZOOM. Make money online teaching trading, stock and forex

ALEXIA SMALL & MARK BROKER

© **Copyright 2020 - All rights reserved.**

The content contained within this book may not be reproduced, duplicated or transmitted without direct written permission from the author or the publisher.

Under no circumstances will any blame or legal responsibility be held against the publisher, or author, for any damages, reparation, or monetary loss due to the information contained within this book. Either directly or indirectly.

Legal Notice:

This book is copyright protected. This book is only for personal use. You cannot amend, distribute, sell, use, quote or paraphrase any part, or the content within this book, without the consent of the author or publisher.

Disclaimer Notice:

Please note the information contained within this document is for educational and entertainment purposes only. All effort has been executed to present accurate, up to date, and reliable, complete information. No warranties of any kind are declared or implied. Readers acknowledge that the author is not engaging in the rendering of legal, financial, medical or professional advice. The content within this book has been derived from various sources. Please consult a licensed professional before attempting any techniques outlined in this book.

By reading this document, the reader agrees that under no circumstances is the author responsible for any losses, direct or indirect, which are incurred as a result of the use of information contained within this document, including, but not limited to, — errors, omissions, or inaccuracies.

TABLE OF CONTENTS

ONLINE TEACHING WITH ZOOM 1

Introduction 2

1. Coronavirus Closed Schools & Academic Institutions 3

    The Impact of Coronavirus on Education   3

    The UN's Report   2

2. How Important is Information Technology and Virtual World is for Teachers and Students 2

3. Different Ways of Teaching Online 8

    Online Video Calls   11

    Live Chats   12

    Web Conferencing   12

    Webinar   13

        Effectiveness of Online Teaching 14

    Guidelines for effective Online Teaching   16

        Interaction 16
        Focus on Active Learning 16
        Make Small Groups 17
        Be Present 17
        Parse Your Time 17
        Embrace Multi-media Assignments 18

4. Why Zoom is the Best Source for Teachers & Academics 19

    Zoom as the Best Teaching Source   19

    Connecting remotely costs less   20

        LMS Integration with Zoom 20
        Source of Earning 21
        High Security 21

Password requirement 21
Require Permission 22
Mute button 22
Zoom App 23
Nonverbal feedback 23
Take live presentations 24
Easy to share a meeting 24
Quality image and audio 24
Ability to share slides and content 25
Annotation tools for everyone 25
Chat feature 26
More control to host 26
Waiting Room 26
Easy to kick out the mischievous students 27
Anyone can be a host 27
Use of pen and pointer 28
Sharing screen without becoming the host 28
Whiteboard 28

5. How to Use ZOOM for Online Learning 30

A Step-by-step Guide to Using Zoom   31

- Logging in 32
- Host a Meeting 32

Meetings   33

6. Some of the Most Interesting Features of Zoom 35
6. Do's and Don'ts of using Zoom at Schools, Colleges & Universities 43

The Do's of Zoom   44

The Don'ts of using Zoom   49

7. How to check Homework and Assignments through Zoom . 55

Why do Institutes choose to Zoom?   55

8. Zoom FAQs for Teachers 63

From where do I download the latest version of Zoom?................................63
How long it will take to download Zoom?..63
What equipment do teachers need for Zoom?..63
How much storage space does Zoom need?..63
Do we need an account to use the Zoom?..64
How to create a Zoom account?..64
Is the Zoom app free?..64
How many participants can join?...64
Is there a training session or guidelines to use this app?...........................65
How a teacher can teach his students to use Zoom?..................................65
Do students need to create a Zoom account to join the class?..................65
Why teachers should use Zoom through canvas?......................................65
How to create a meeting?...65
How to invite students to the class meeting?...66
Can I use my meeting ID to create a meeting?..66
How do I schedule a meeting in the future?..66
How can students join a meeting?...66
Can we get the Zoom plugin /add-on for Microsoft Outlook?..................66
Can you create a meeting of students more than 300?...............................67
Who can edit the Zoom meeting details?..67
How to take class attendance in Zoom?..67
What do I need if I'm using Zoom outside of Canvas?.............................67
Can I use a Bluetooth headset?..68
How to connect the audio on Zoom?...68
Can you mute or unmute your participants?...68
How to take notes while taking a Zoom class?...68
If a class has students more than 40 or 60, can I be able to see them simultaneously?..69
Can participant change other participants setting?...................................69
Can we teach on Zoom without turning on the camera?...........................69
Can we share documents on Zoom?..69
Can we share photos and videos?..70
Can we share the URL on Zoom?...70
Can we write on the Zoom screen or page?..70
How to share the screen on the Zoom?...70
How to share screens from the second camera?.......................................70
How can we share our Zoom window and toolbar?..................................71
What annotation tool can teachers use?..71
Can students become a host?...71

Can we make co-host? 71
Who can raise a hand in Zoom? 71
Can students share the screen without becoming a host? 72
What else can students share on Zoom without becoming a host?............ 72
How to record my lectures on Zoom? 72
Can students record the Zoom meeting on the cloud?............................... 72
How much space is need for a one-hour recording? 72
Why I don't have a record button on the control option?........................... 72
Can students chat with teachers?.. 73
Can participants chat with each other?.. 73
Can the host see the chat of participants?.. 73
Does the host have access to stop the private chat between the students? .73
Is it a host choice to let anyone enter the meeting? 73
Can the host be allowed to lock the meeting? 74
How to use the breakout rooms? 74
Can the host do the polling during the meeting?....................................... 74
How many questions can be asked on polls? 74
Are Q&A sessions only available on webinars? 74
If a teacher only wants their students to see them when they are saying something, what should they do?.. 74

Conclusion 76
STOCK MARKET INVESTING 78
FOR BEGINNERS 78
MARK BROKER 78
Introduction... 81
1. The ABC of Stock Market 83

What Is The Stock Market?   84

Who Integrates It?   84

Role of the Stock Exchange   85

How Does The Stock Market Work?   85

Can I Invest In The Stock Market From Home?   87

Invest in the stock market: What platform to use?   88

How much money do I have to invest in the stock market?	89
Can I start investing in a stock simulator?	90

2. The Mechanics of Owning, Buying and Selling Stocks 91

Buy Shares to Become A Shareholder — 91

- Buy and sell stocks with online brokers 92
- Purchase and sale orders for shares 93

When is it the best time to buy shares on the stock exchange? — 93

- When is it a good idea to sell the shares on the stock exchange? 94
- How long do you have to hold stocks in a short-term strategy? 95
- How long do you have to keep stocks in a long-term strategy? 96
- When should the shares be resold? 96
- What shares can be purchased or sold online? 97
- What stocks to invest in? 97

3. Who is a Broker & How to Choose One 99

Stockbroker: What is it? — 99

- Stockbroker: Functions 100
- Characteristics of a Stockbroker 100
- How to choose the right stockbroker? 101

A Background Check Is a Must — 101

- Interviewing multiple runners is a must. 102
- Check out these red flags. 103
- Do your homework with references. 104

4. How to Assess Risk and Volatility 105

- Individual risk assessment 105
- Systematic risk assessment 106
- Standard Deviation 107
- Beta 107
- Value at risk 107
- Conditional Value at risk 107

What is Volatility? — 108

	Implied Volatility	110
	Historical Volatility	111
5.	**Top Indicators of a Winning Investment**	**113**
	Trend line	113
	Simple Moving Average	114
	Rate of change	115
	Relative strength Index	116
	Moving Average Convergence Divergence	117
	Bollinger Bands	118
	Fibonacci Retracements	119
	All about Technical Indicators	120
6.	**Basic Investment Techniques**	**124**
	10 Basic Investment Techniques for Beginners	125
7.	**What You Should Know About Taxes**	**132**
	The Long-term Capital Gains Rate Criteria	133
	Reducing Tax on your Stock Sales	133
	Experimenting with the Wash Rule	135
	Deduction of Capital Losses	136
	Other Deductible Expenses in Investment	136
	Final verdict	137
8.	**All about the Bull & Bear Market**	**139**
	High Gross Domestic Products	140
	Rising Stock Prices	141
	Longer Stock Trading	141
	Lower Unemployment Rates	141
	The Bull Market History	141
	The Bear Market Indicators	143
	The Bear Market History	144
9.	**Common stock exchange terms and what they mean**	**146**
	What is the Stock Market?	146
	1-Annual Report	147

2- Arbitrage 147
3- Averaging Down 147
4- Bear Market 148
5- Bull Market 148
6- Beta 148
7- Blue Chip Stocks 148
8- Bourse 149
9- Broker 149
10- Bid 149
11- Close 149
12- Day trading 150
13- Dividend 150
14- Exchange 150
15- Execution 150
16- Haircut 151
17- High 151
18- Initial Public Offering 151
19- Leverage 151
20- Low 152
21- Margin 152
22- Moving Average 152
23- Open 152
24- Order 153
25- pink sheet stocks 153
26- Sector 153

10.   Tips and tricks for investing in the Stock Exchange ... 154
1- Invest in Index Fund 154
2- Focus on Mutual Funds 155
3- Timing the Market 155
4- Set Goals 155
5- Five Golden steps of trading to learn: 156
6- Have a balance of investments 156
7- Think for long term 157
8- Buy value stocks 157
9- Diversify investments among sectors 157
10- How much risk you can take? 158
11- Control your emotions 158
12- 360 Degree View 158
13- Automate stocks 159

14- Say no to leverage 159
15- Choose one sector 159
16- Risk vs. Return 159
17- Buy low sell higher 160
Final Word 160

Conclusion 162

INTRODUCTION

"Teaching in the Internet age means we must teach tomorrow's skills today." - Jennifer Fleming

According to a UNESCO report, many governments had temporarily closed educational institutes of all kinds in pursuit of containing the spread of the Coronavirus pandemic.

This worldwide closure impacted over 60 percent of the student population. Many countries instigated domestic closures affecting millions of new learners.

This situation had, no doubt, a drastic impact!

With schools closed down, millions of students lost the opportunity to acquire knowledge; billions became deprived of attaining their degrees in the year (2020), and without their degrees completed, many lost the opportunity to land into the right job for them.

Under this situation, governments took a good initiative. They decided to start classes remotely so that students do not suffer (anymore), thanks to IT. It (remote learning & teaching) offers many benefits:

- Quick and a fast way to get connected
- Saves time
- Cost-effective (since it saves transportation cost)
- Easy to use

Now a question arises – how does this work? The answer, you must (already be) familiar with is through different websites and apps – and one such (effective) app is Zoom!

With more than 12 million monthly subscribers by 2002, Zoom has become one of the most used and most reliable Video Conferencing apps for everyone. Not just teachers and academics – people from all walks of life trust this app.

Learn more about the pros, uses, advantageous features of this app in this Ebook.

Enjoy home-based learning with Zoom!

1. CORONAVIRUS CLOSED SCHOOLS & ACADEMIC INSTITUTIONS

According to a famous Chinese proverb, if someone wants to plan for a year, they should sow rice; if they want to plan for a decade, they should plant trees. And if they want to plan for a lifetime – go for educating people!

What if governments stop schools and other institutions from functioning anymore?

Sounds strange? Not anymore….

Students and teachers faced this issue actually this year (2020) in the wake of the Coronavirus pandemic.

The Impact of Coronavirus on Education

The Covid-19 pandemic has led to a near-total closure of educational institutes worldwide, recently. Although the institutes are reopening slowly with time, the impact it left is HUGE!

The pandemic, as of July 2020, affected more than 1.7 billion students worldwide. UNICEF stated in a report that a total number of 106 countries implemented the cease (of educational institutes). This impacted 98 percent of the international student population.

Cambridge International Examinations (CIE) had also canceled their examinations – like for SAT, A and O levels, and more.

The closure impact not only pupils, families, and teachers; but have deep societal and economic outcomes. Some notable issue that showed up includes homelessness, student debt, food insecurity, digital learning, and more.

This effect was severer on underprivileged children and their parents. It took away their opportunity to seek education at all.

Other consequences of the school closures caused:

- Increase in the number of dropouts
- Disengagement in learning
- The strain on the healthcare system
- Food and nutrition insecurity
- Disruption in all types of education providing services (like vocational and technical training, skills development, and more)

Besides, the most common cause is the idea and implementation of remote learning.

The UN's Report

A report by the United Nations was released in August 2020 on the above topic. According to that report, "The pandemic has caused the 'largest disruption of the education system in history.'

This report also states that the disruption in the education system has worsened the pre-existing issue of education for the underprivileged. The problem has further shrunken the learning opportunities for many vulnerable children.

UN called it the 'Learning Loss' in the report. Un says that 'learning losses' threatened generations and have erased the decades of progress – especially for girls and young females who wanted to study. About 23.8 million (additional) students are 'feared' to drop out or lose access to school in the upcoming years due to coronavirus' (long-term) effects.

Now one must think would this impact go away?

UN answers: The coronavirus impact is 'far from over.' This is a learning crisis that would impact generations and generations!

This situation calls for an urgent action without which the impact would continue to spread. Out of many solutions, one of the best solutions given and implemented by many countries is the initiation of classes remotely. Students, no matter where they are, can learn any subject via the internet.

This solution is not only cost-effective, but it also saves time. It can also help keep children engaged even when they cannot go out of home or have limited activity. Moreover, another 'great' benefit of remote learning is it helps children and students to stay focused on their studies and use the internet more positively (instead of playing games, engaging in social media activities, and waste their precious time.)

In simple words, it means, remote learning also helps keep children away from the 'negative' effects of using the internet. In fact, it is an out-of-the-box solution that allows children to learn, interact (with their teachers and fellows) without getting bored.

In the end, we would like to recall a quote from a known US-based educationist, Rosalie Ledda Valdez. She says, let us think out of the box and try to create an interactive and useful learning experience for students.

This (quote) can be applied to recover the losses made in the wake of the Coronavirus, can't we?

2. HOW IMPORTANT IS INFORMATION TECHNOLOGY AND VIRTUAL WORLD IS FOR TEACHERS AND STUDENTS

In 2016, the Education Commission presented a report at a conference of the world leaders. Educationists and policymakers set up to investigate how to deliver education for all children by 2030.

This report said: if we want to equip our children and youngsters with skills and knowledge – we need far-reaching innovation. We need to educate more and more children using new technology and make them more empowered.

Importance of Information Technology

Anyone would agree that technology is changing us. Not only us but our lives too!

It has revolutionized the whole world; some consider it bad, and some consider it a useful thing. But I think it all depends on your own perspective, how you perceive things.

According to the older generation, technology, particularly smartphones, TV, video games, has ruined the millennial. But in reality, technology is not the enemy here. Technology has made our lives easier. Technology is the real game now.

Reaching somebody who is living 2000 miles away from you is only a click away. News travels faster than before. The advancement of science has made over the past few years are remarkable. The cure and vaccines to different diseases are here. You can reach anywhere you want in less time. Especially time, technology saves time. Like tasks that used to take up days and hours; can easily be solved within minutes now.

Education in Emergencies

There had been several deadly plagues and epidemics throughout human history, but during those times, who could imagine still passing a class or earning? I am not saying that COVID19 did not affect the economic system of the world; it has greatly has changed the economic system, but as compared to the old ones, people still managed to attend their classes and work, and it was possible only due to the advancements in technology. Without access to the online world or IT, the world would have suffered a great deal.

I, for one, believe that rather than condemning Technology, it's time for everyone to embrace and appreciate the advances it has made. The betterment it has bought into our lives. It is not something one should fear or bash, but it should be celebrated.

Technology and Education

Technology and its relation to today's education. As I mentioned earlier, that technology has an impact on our daily lives even more than we realize. We are dependent on technology in more than one way.

Just like that, technology has affected education too. The advancement in teaching methods! The level and competition in education are higher than ever.

Technology is a huge resource for students. It provides them with the world's views and articles and books, anywhere from the world.

In older times, only a few had access to books and teachers but now. Everything is one click away, all the E-books are available online, and there are dozens of videos available worldwide for lessons and different things.

Can Technology Deliver Education?

In schools around the world, Technology infuses classrooms with digital learning tools, i.e., Laptop, Smartphone, projector, etc., expands course offerings, experiences, and learning materials; supports learning 24 hours a day, seven days a week.

Technology has introduced us to new teaching methods.

It helps you build new technological skills; increases student engagement because students like to be interactive and are accustomed to new technologies; they are a part of their daily lifestyle, so using technology in your classroom increases student's interests and motivation to not only learn but to explore new things.

Technology skills

Believe it or not, but students need technological skills. Most of the jobs will not even exist in the near future since the whole world is being shifted to technology. These skills are important to play a role in the international world.

Without our young generation knowing how to use or handle technology or the internet, their education would be of no use. And by technology, I do not only mean tech services but in other fields as well. In medicine, doctors need to know how to operate new devices. For a businessman, it's important to handle his business online since most of the businesses have been shifted to the online marketing side; teachers should know how to use teaching applications and new innovative teaching methods, it is important for their effective teaching.

Teachers and Technology

Technology has transformed teaching. It has ushered a new model for educationists. This links teachers with their students and enables them to keep in touch with each other all the time. Thanks to technology, it also has helped improved the way teaching methods and learning were perceived in the world.

Teachers used to be the primary and only source of learning, but since the advancement, in Technology, it deems necessary for the teachers now to use tools for the improved version of the learning environment.

Technology makes teaching easy

We all have been there. How many times during your lecture and class, you were actually paying attention to the teacher? Most of the time, students are lost in their own thoughts. It's not because "they are dumb" or "wasting money" but because usually, they lose the grip of the lecture, or most teachers cannot keep the students' interest in the present. Now, how do you solve this problem?

You simply cannot kick every student out of the class or start labeling them. It simply does not work.

Teachers can also find ways to make their lesson plans and lectures more interesting and more effective. Technology has made it easier for them to deliver lessons in a more 'meaningful' way.

With the help of video and audio presentation! And with the help of technical knowledge, it can be put into practice…

Information is Accessible

Technology has made everything accessible for not only teachers but students as well. Imagine spending hours in the library and looking for the required information or book.

It was very time-consuming. Technology has made everything very accessible. You can easily find out your required articles, news, and books online.

Teachers can easily access their assignments and work. They can also keep track of them through various different online applications.

There is Google classroom for remote attendance, grading, and keeping your assignments in check along with online video and audio classroom service. My students' progress is the application that helps teachers keeps track of their students' progress.

Zoom app is another tool that helps students interact vastly. They can share their assignments, create their own personal classroom meetings, and keep track of time as well.

With online teaching, students can write better and longer articles and research because A, their hands do not get tired by all the writing.

B, they can contain more data online because international news is also available to them. In fact, they can gather interviews from all over the world by just sitting in one place.

C, with the help of online tools like Grammarly, Turnitin can check their mistakes before submitting their assignments.

In fact, schools and colleges can build up their own learning portal. In fact, most of the colleges even have during COVID19.

The benefit of building your own portal is that you can personalize it. Change its interface; however, one deems fit.

Learning is fun now

Technology has made learning experience for students more enjoyable. Everyone is into social media these days. Facebook, Instagram, Pinterest, etc. as these applications can distract them from the learning process, but if used correctly, it can be helpful inclination to spend time online for the education process as well: Making learning more fun.

Apply the latest touch-screen technology to make the lessons more interactive. You can also use memes and interesting online posts to teach something nice to your students. Use different interactive apps and games to initiate a discussion or increase student involvement. Set up different social media groups for your pupils and inspire them to constructive conversations.

3. DIFFERENT WAYS OF TEACHING ONLINE

Once Heidi-Hayes said, teachers should integrate technology seamlessly into their curriculum. They should not think of it as an add-on, an afterthought, or something not good for the students – and it is true!

Importance of Online Applications

Remote education is very convenient, especially for the students and teachers who have to manage more than one task in their lives. And in this recent economy, most of the students are working as well as managing their studies, and with online education, it can easily be managed.

Even for the teachers or students who have young kids or cannot manage to go to college, online education helps them in scheduling their time and work more conveniently.

According to a report, admission for online courses is higher, with more than six million students taking at least one online course. However, the dropout rate is also high for online students than for students in traditional classroom settings. What prompts students to drop these online courses?

According to the survey, it is because teachers and even students are not really familiar with online applications. They do not really have hands-on experience with these things.

How can you deliver education if you yourself are not familiar with the mode you are using to deliver?

Learning online applications for teachers is necessary. Especially for the recent teaching system!

The online education system also saves money. Previously in traditional classrooms, we spent thousands of dollars setting up video conferencing rooms and equipment, and often participants had equipment failures or inadequate visibility.

Faculty needed the presence of a technical support person to run the equipment and maintenance, which meant that advanced scheduling and coordination often limited spontaneity or usage. Usually, a successful setup took at least fifteen minutes, and instructors found that a connection might drop mid-conference.

Frustrated with the technology, the need for support, and the loss of class time, electricity bills, accommodating students in one place, then in the case of pandemic or emergency and traffic also a part of a hurdle, many faculty abandoned these systems altogether.

In order to ignore all these mishaps and unfortunate events, It is important for the teachers to know the importance of online apps and should have hands-on experience about them.

There are different ways of online teaching. Some of them are explained below:

Professional teaching courses are not limited only to content delivery techniques. These courses can also be combined with additional technologies for the learners. The following are just some of these tools that support some real-time communication:

- Video platforms
- Live chats, individual or course-wise
- Web conferencing
- Telephonic Lessons
- Virtual meetings
- Downloadable pre-recorded lectures
- Microsoft PowerPoint presentations with or without voice-over
- Forums and discussion boards
- Email communication
- Teaching via Google & other collaborative tools
- Tools for 24-hour support, like virtual resource centers and video tutoring
- Audio Lessons
- Slide sharing
- Online testing etc.

Each of these tools encourages live participation and interaction, although also let you record the live sessions so that in case if you miss your class, you still have the material available for you. And it does not leave students behind from one another.

Online Video Calls

Probably the latest and one of the best ways to teach students is through online video conferencing. There are many apps and websites out there that provide this service. One such platform is ZOOM!

Zoom is a great invention. It is not only useful for college and teaching purposes but also for office use.

Features of Zoom app

- You can voice call or video call on Zoom with the help of your personal Zoom meeting room.
- You can add as many people as you want.
- You can schedule your meetings.
- You can join and create a meeting with a simple click.
- You can record your Zoom meeting.
- You can also chat with everyone or an individual privately.
- You can share your screen with anyone and also allow the other participant to share theirs.
- You can attach, send, and receive documents and pictures on a Zoom meeting.

- It also has a cute feature of "raise hand" in its chatbox – Which can be helpful in voting or virtual attendance!

These are just a few basic features of the Zoom app. It is a self-explanatory app. You can also just download it and check out for yourself or maybe run a mock session. It is also very helpful.

Live Chats

Live chats with bots or real people are not (something) new. Companies use this technique for customer interaction. Educational institutes, however, can also use it for student-teacher interaction. They can either chat on a one-to-one basis or in groups. Whatsapp group chat can be a great option.

- Teachers can create student groups
- Sharing of files, homework, and another assignment is possible
- Audio lectures can be delivered instantly
- Video calling for tests is also possible
- Combine study on Whatsapp groups is a good option if someone (student) is stuck at a point.

Web Conferencing

A web conference is a form of a virtual meeting. In that, students (and other people) from different places can exchange their ideas, knowledge, and information in real-time.

Web conferencing is also an effective way to teach online. Students sitting anywhere in the world can join the conference and learn new things.

Web conferencing is specifically used for interactive learning and training sessions. It brings together different people in the same way as a conference call works. It has multiple features like:

- Multimedia sharing
- Online polls
- Live question/answer sessions
- Screen sharing
- Live question and answer session
- Real-time interaction

Another version of the web conference is webinar and webcast. See more on the webinar below.

Webinar

The webinar, just like the name indicates, is a seminar but through the web. It is an online conference or presentation app.

Features of Webinar

- You can use audio and video calling through webinars.

- It also gives you the option to live chat with other participants.

- It also allows the participants to use the microphone for their queries during the live session.

- One webinar session can host more than 500 participants.

- It helps with the easy presentation of slideshows, documents, and screen content

- You can share, download, and record complete lectures and share or view them afterward.

- There are three types of webinars; Live Webinars, on-Demand Webinars, and automated Webinars.

- It also gives you the opportunity to surveys, polls, MCQs, exams, and quizzes

Effectiveness of Online Teaching

For the first time, online teachers require some time to adjust. During the first three days, you should take the trail. Teachers should prepare their lessons well even if it Is for a virtual audience. They should assess how well their teaching technique is working and adapt it accordingly.

Professional classroom-based courses can help evaluate instructional success through testing and assessments. You can also check this out by questioning your students, taking their feedbacks.

If you are still unsure, rehearse your lesson. Online recordings are possible, right!

'E-teachers' can also evaluate various teaching techniques via assessments and student interactions. However, be sure that the data-driven nature of technology gives a less subjective measurement of success.

You should also learn online management systems. This will help you monitor students' progress and learning behaviors. You can then compile your report and add reviews online.

Teachers can also monitor how often students log in, how much time they spend on different tasks and assignments, and how well they are absorbing the material.

This type of tracking is valuable!

Such monitoring earning can help teachers instantly spot the major areas of concern. This makes them adjust their teaching techniques accordingly. Teachers can also modify their teaching material and keep it updated from time to time.

Teachers new to online instruction can benefit from more guidance in this area from online resources and through different apps. Besides, they should not hesitate to find the support they need.

If you do not know how to use an application, do not hesitate to ask others. There is nothing wrong with asking.

Trust me, your students will respect you. Because there are very few teachers or professors that students remember for the rest of their life, be friendly with your students. Because a friendly teacher transcends their position in your life — they turn a chemistry or algebra lesson into an opportunity to teach you how to learn. And no matter how successful a student gets in their life, they will always remember that one teacher with all their heart.

Guidelines for effective Online Teaching

Here are a few guidelines for teachers for effective online teaching;

Interaction

• Firstly, interact with your students. Try not to start teaching directly. Get to know your class first. Ask some ice-breaking questions.

Focus on Active Learning

• According to Conrad, "Teachers often rely on long lectures to fill the time in a traditional class meeting. But even the most dynamic lecturers cannot get away with that online."

• To make the lecture interesting and engaging, mix spurts of discussions, collaboration, video and audio clips, and hands-on exercises with text and possibly brief videos and ppt.

Make Small Groups

- The academic director of Loyola University Maryland's said in an interview, we deal with different kinds of students. Mostly, introverts or shy ones do not participate in discussions or ask questions. That participation is necessary but can be equally intimidating if students are expected to engage with dozens of classmates.

- Making small groups. It is beneficial for both students and teachers. Since they will get to know each other better, it is easier to coordinate with smaller groups.

Be Present

- According to Boettcher, of Designing for Learning, "No matter where teaching and learning take place, the importance of the faculty member being there and being mentally present with the students is the most important thing they can do."

- It does not simply mean that it starts responding to every question. But have a special presence in the online classroom. She suggested faculty members build a proper online profile.

- "Students should have a well-rounded idea of who [their professors are] as people," Boettcher said.

Parse Your Time

You do not have to respond to every query 24 7. Manage your time. Spend an hour a day to respond to every email or query. You do not have to be available all the time

Sometimes, teaching online can consume you completely. So, you still need to take some personal time out for yourself!

Embrace Multi-media Assignments

- Students in online classes usually are at least somewhat familiar with the technology.

- Teachers should leverage that by allowing them to use digital tools for their assignments. Let them experiment with different tools or videos to present. Let them show their creativity. As long as they are getting that knowledge, there is nothing wrong with them experimenting with different tools.

4. WHY ZOOM IS THE BEST SOURCE FOR TEACHERS & ACADEMICS

Due to the coronavirus pandemic, all the schools, colleges, and universities were closed, and to connect them remotely and continue the studies, it was Zoom who helped every department. Even people started using the Zoom to have their office meetings to get things on track. This was the main reason that Zoom gained so much popularity in those days.

The greatest benefit of using Zoom is that you can have 100 participants in a single meeting without buying a premium package, and this is the main reason because of which almost all of the universities and colleges preferred Zoom for virtual classes.

On the other hand, Zoom also faced some security issues, but for now, it is fully updated, and Zoom has tried to be best in keeping people privacy safe, and you can do this by applying different security settings as recommended by Zoom.

Zoom as the Best Teaching Source

Zoom is indeed the best tool for teachers and academics (and, of course, for educational institutions). Here is how:

Connecting remotely costs less

One of the greatest advantages of Zoom for teachers is that they can connect to their students remotely from anywhere in the world. It just requires an internet connection, and they are good to go, which costs low.

If they have to reach physically somewhere daily, it will cost them a lot. Teachers in the coronavirus pandemic were able to take their classes by the comfort of their homes, and this also not affected their monthly salary.

LMS Integration with Zoom

Webinars are always the most recommended and effective way of delivering content for learning purposes. This helps learners to easily understand the topic visualize the scenario. To streamline training webinars, universities and colleges can easily integrate Zoom with LMS, which is a blessing for the teachers. This also helps to save a lot of extra work and time.

You can save and schedule a session in LMS, and it will be automatically uploaded and updated on Zoom too. So you will save a lot of admin work. When you create a session, all your participants are enrolled, and also they receive a notification on their mail with the time and date of the session to be held. So they can also set a reminder not to forget.

Source of Earning

Zoom has also become a source of earning platform for the teachers. Teachers have started taking classes related to different courses. Everyone knows that students are always willing to do a short course to have a grip on some digital skills. One of the greatest examples is Udemy and Coursera, where teachers are earning thousands of dollars monthly, and students love to enroll in premium courses there to have a skill.

High Security

Well, if we are involved in Internet things, there is always a high risk of security because we are never aware of where it's safe to share our personal information or where it's a high risk. So we easily get trapped by the hackers and get scammed.

Some years back, Zoom security was also very weak, and people face real trouble using this conference calling website. But with time, Zoom has now made sure to tighten their security and have updated its website according to the latest trends. Teachers or the meeting host is given a lot of freedom to set security layers to avoid any disturbance in the class. One of the perfect examples is the password required to enter into a meeting.

Password requirement

As stated above, Zoom has now worked on its security, and now you can tighten your security according to your requirements if you are a host. When you are a host, Zoom allows you to manage settings and make people suffer who want to distract your meetings.

If you are the host, you can enable meeting password required privacy settings, and anyone who wants to enter your meeting will have to know the password first. So you can share your meeting password to only those participants whom you want to enter in your meeting.

Require Permission

Zoom is now becoming the most used platform for conference calls, and it's giving a tough time to its main competitor Skype.

One of the reasons for Zoom's popularity is its advanced security patterns. The host is given so much freedom to control meeting according to his or her willingness. If you are a teacher, your first preference would always be to make sure that there should be no disturbance in the class.

To make it happen, you can manage your settings to require permission to enter the meeting. Now, this is a really helpful feature for teachers. They can allow only those students in their meetings who are known to them. So no anonymous user can enter the meeting to create any disturbance.

Mute button

One of the biggest problems of online classes is distractions because of participants' background noise. Zoom allows the meeting host to mute all the microphones of their participants, so there will be no more issues regarding the background noise of the meeting attendants. Students also misuse the microphone feature, and to avoid this from happening, all teachers should always consider mute students' microphones.

Zoom App

Zoom is the best source for teachers and academics because Zoom also has its official app for both Android and IOS users. So whether the teachers are traveling or having a trip with their family, they can connect remotely with their students with the help of mobile phones within seconds.

Zoom app is free to use, whether you are using an Android or an IOS user. You can connect 100 participants from anywhere in the world without having to buy premium packages, which are almost enough if you are using it to take a class.

Nonverbal feedback

When we are physically present in the classroom, we are always asked by the teacher to raise a hand if they have any question or clap if someone did good in class in accordance to appreciate him or her. To help out, teachers, Zoom has added these gestures as icons in the chat feature.

So, students can raise a hand if they want to ask a question by clicking on raise hand, and it will show in chat. Students can also use a clap icon, thumbs up icon according to the situation to act upon it. This helps to maximize the engagement level of the participants and also helps teachers to understand the behavior of the class.

Take live presentations

There are hundreds of benefits for teachers using Zoom, including being able to make presentations online. Teachers can easily take live presentations of students, and by applying Zoom security settings, they can open the cam and mic of a student who is presenting. Teachers can take both audio, video presentations according to their requirements.

Zoom also helps someone willing for group presentations. As all the control is in the hands of the meeting host, who will be your teacher, can go through the settings and open the cam or microphone of the students who are in a group.

Easy to share a meeting

Zoom app provides access to share your meeting. When you create the meeting, you want to share it with your students, and Zoom gives plenty of options to share the meeting. You can share your Zoom meeting on different platforms so that students can join it easily. You simply have to copy the link to share it. The students can also share the further if they want to. Overall it's easy for teachers to share the link of Zoom class.

Quality image and audio

Another reason for academics to use this app is its quality voice and image. The Zoom app shows a good quality image. Whatever you share, on-screen is displayed mostly in its best quality. It does not change the quality of the image. The students can see the quality image of slides.

The voice quality of this app is best. The teacher's voice can be heard clearly without any interruption. No complaint of interference. The host and participants can speak, hear each other voices.

Ability to share slides and content

The main reason to use such apps is that you can share the slides or the content you want to teach during the live session. The teacher and students can talk to each other to understand things better, but the Zoom app provides the facility to share the slides on the screen which you are teaching.

When the content they are learning is in front of their eyes, then they can learn it more easily. The students understand the slides well in this way. It's easy for teachers to teach them by sharing it on screen. Teachers can share documents and photos.

Annotation tools for everyone

The Zoom provides the annotation tools. You can make highlights the text or the same figure on the image. You can pointer or mark on the slide which you are sharing; we can also erase the marks.

The feature can be used by both teachers and students. The host and participants had the facility to use these features. It is helpful for teachers when they are teaching students a specific slide; they have to point on the exact location to tell the students what they are saying. It is one big feature that this app provides.

Chat feature

The Zoom has a helpful chat feature. You can share documents and other important information using it. The Zoom participants can also read and write, talk, discuss a topic, and initiate a debate through this app.

All the participants can talk to each other; you can send messages to anyone who joins the meeting. No need to use another app for chat. The Zoom app provides enough features which we need for a chat. The chat of the Zoom app is widely used for sharing documents and important information. Adding the chat function in the app make it more superior!

More control to host

Usually, the teacher is the host of the meeting, which makes him in charge of the class. The host can control the class. The host can turn off the microphone of any student; the host can kick out anyone or allow anyone to enter the class. It means this gives more power to teachers. It's better to control the class when you have such functions.

Waiting Room

The Waiting Room is such an incredible option that this app has. This allows you to know who is entering your class. This security feature lets you know who is joining the meeting, whether he/she is in your class or not. This is a big problem that some other people join the meeting who are not even part of the institution.

This waiting room function of Zoom has solved this problem by checking whether he is your student or not. The host will see and allow only the students who are part of the class. It secures our class.

Easy to kick out the mischievous students

The Zoom app provides the ability to host to kick out the mischievous students. During the class, the students make a disturbance; not all students create the problem; it's the few ones that are not interested in studying.

It's easy for a teacher to kick such students out and then simply continue his class. This act usually happens with teachers when they are teaching, but the teachers have the option to remove them or mute them. In this way, it's good for them to continue the class and to avoid these bullies.

Anyone can be a host

During class, when the students have to share something or he/she has to present something, then the student doesn't have to create a new meeting and then share its link with everyone. The host simply has to transfer the host function to that student who has to present.

A teacher can also make a student/co-teacher the host by just enabling that option. They simply have to click on it for this purpose. This saves you from wasting your time in creating a new meeting – just transfer it to someone else. That's it! This is an amazing function that the Zoom app offers.

Use of pen and pointer

During the class, it's not just the host who is allowed to use the tools or annotation. All the participants can use these tools. The pen and pointer are useful tools that Zoom provides.

You can ask teachers by using the pointer to point on a specific line to repeat it, or you don't understand it. The students can use tools for their understanding of some topic or during class when they are talking to their teacher about it. It is quite a helpful tool for teachers and students.

Sharing screen without becoming the host

The students can share the screen without becoming the host. In this way, the host has control of the class, and the students can share their screen. This is quite a good feature for academics. It's easy for students to share their screens by just enabling the option. The screen share also provides the annotation tools to the students. You can also create figures using these tools while sharing the screen.

Whiteboard

The Zoom app provides another amazing feature, which is the whiteboard. This feature is very helpful for teachers and students, especially for mathematics teachers. It allows you to write on the screen by using different tools. It has a white screen.

Teachers can explain mathematics, science, or physics problems on it and explain more complex topics without issues. Mostly, it is used when a teacher needs aboard to write and explain it to their students.

The whiteboard features give a real-time 'classroom' feeling!

5. HOW TO USE ZOOM FOR ONLINE LEARNING

Even those who never had worked online before; those who never even touched their digital devices for teaching or learning – are increasingly using ZOOM nowadays. Let alone teachers, in fact, people from all walks of life – are on ZOOM.

Here are some instances:

Mr. Smith is a 55-years-old psychiatrist from Wales. He spent all his life treating patients at a local hospital (near his house). The situation, however, took a different turn in 2020. Hospitals had to close OPDs in the wake of the new Coronavirus. This left Mr. Smith in awe.

He had to sit back home for many months – and do nothing. No patient could come near (due to social distancing), and his wife also insisted (him) to stay at home. One day he met with a fellow doctor who was using online means to treat patients.

Impressed by the solution, Mr. Smith also contacted his assistant to help him learn using ZOOM.

Similarly, Martha is also a teacher at a school in Turkey. The year 2020 proved to be a bad year for her. She lost her job in a foreign land. The closure of schools made her go back to her hometown, empty-handed.

Stressed out and anxious to get a job, she created an online group and started taking coaching classes online.

Martha is not penniless (empty-handed) anymore!

A Step-by-step Guide to Using Zoom

Did you know how many people can take a Zoom class online?

The answer is 100!

Isn't it amazing? This simply means teachers wishing to take a joint session can also use Zoom without a problem.

Here is how you can start using Zoom if you are new to this app.

Zoom is a useful 'free' calling platform. You can access it from anywhere – a tablet, laptop, or smartphone.

First of all, download Zoom from an app store (if you are using an iOS phone, visit the Apple store; otherwise, check out Playstore for android.

Visit the Zoom website to download it for your machine (computer/laptop).

Then,

Now it is time to launch the App. You will see this screen once you get there:

"Join a Meeting" or "Sign In"

New users, however, should create a fresh account. It is free! Use your Facebook or Google account to Sign up.

If you wish to use Zoom for your school/educational institute, chances are Zoom can get you a special (school/institute) domain.

- **Logging in**

After logging in, you can join, create, or schedule a meeting.

Join a Meeting

To join a meeting, the App asks you to enter your meeting ID or add the 'Personal link name.' Then, hit join.

P.S. Make sure the meeting host has allowed you to that specific meeting.

- **Host a Meeting**

To become a meeting host, you will see three options in the drop-down menu.

1. with video on

2. with video off

3. Screen share only

As their names suggest, 'with video on' means your video will be turned on automatically. While for video off, you would not be able to show your video to the meeting participants. The third option is 'screen share only.'

Once you click on any of the above options, you would land on the 'Meetings' page.

Meetings

On the meetings section, a menu appears that contains options like: "Upcoming," "Previous," "Personal Room," and "Meeting Templates." Here you can schedule a meeting, set time duration, and check the previous meeting details.

To get the details of your Meeting room, go to "Personal Room." You can also save meeting templates here (in that section).

One of the best things about Zoom is it offers step by step training to the users. It also allows for saving recordings for future use. This specific feature is very handy for teachers. It is because they can save their lectures and lessons online with Zoom.

Training Resources

Zoom offers training resource videos for its users. It is a great thing when you get stuck somewhere during the use.

Moreover, one can try out 'test call' by using Zoom. There is customer support also available, just in case you feel stuck.

In conclusion, Zoom is a user-friendly, simple, and fast application that anyone can use – anytime, anywhere!

6. SOME OF THE MOST INTERESTING FEATURES OF ZOOM

There are so many reasons why out of a dozen online applications and tools. It is currently being utilized by more than 6,000 educational institutions around the globe. Why "Zoom" is the top priority for teachers or any other conference, what are its interesting features for the teachers – see below.

Pedagogical Considerations for Teaching with Zoom

Why Zoom is the best source for Teachers? It is closely related to traditional classes. With Zoom, you can implement many teaching methods that you use in traditional classes.

Zoom was specially built for Educational Purposes

You can create your personal "meeting room." To add people and they can also join by the "link," and then it is up to the host if he or she allows them into their meeting room or not.

It is designed with MPEG-4 cloud recording, closed captioning, audio sharing during screen sharing, chat, group messaging, mobile collaboration with co-annotation, among many other features to help make the most of the lessons.

Screen Sharing

Due to Zoom's screen sharing feature, teachers can easily teach with the help of PowerPoint presentations and slides as a part of their lecture.

Control Screen Sharing

The host can share it with a screen, and so can participants. Hos has the option to control the screen sharing process. It can enable the students to share their screens.

Muting Option

Well, every teacher has been there. If students start talking unnecessarily or disturbing the environment, Zoom has just the perfect feature for you. You can now hush them with the "mute" option.

Allows Voting

Zoom allows the participants to "raise hands." there is an option in the chat window where all the participants can raise or not raise their hands. Who would have thought voting would be easier with Zoom?

Stable Connection

No matter how fast your internet is. Every once a while, you do face a connection problem. Either it can be from your end or from the back.

Keeping in mind, Zoom has built its app with a stable connection.

Schedule your Session

How many times have you missed your class or some important meeting? Simply, it is because it slipped through our mind or for any other reason. It happens with all of us. At least once in our lifetime!

Now with Zoom, you can schedule your meetings before. So when the time comes, it will remind you so that you do not have to miss any important meeting or class!

Time

Zoom time feature allows you to host a meeting for 40 minutes (in its free version); you can obviously opt for the premium version where you can host a meeting for as long as you want.

But in its free version meeting ends after 40 minutes. You can join back again using the same meeting link. But it ends on its own after 40 minutes, so you do not have to spend extra hours in a meeting or lecture.

This feature was specially built, keeping in mind the standard lecture time.

Breakout Room

Zoom Breakout room is an interesting and unique feature. In the breakout room, you can split your Zoom session into 50 different rooms. And make a group of participants and divide them.

The host can actually check-in with the participants from time to time in their breakout rooms. It is helpful for group projects, discussions, or quiz.

Invitation

Participants or host does not need to share their private information on Zoom. An email invitation, link, or meeting code can help them join the meeting room.

Remove a Participant

Just like the traditional classroom where you can banish students from the class for one reason or another, you can remove participants from the Zoom application as well.

Control Chat

The host has the option to control chat options. Teachers can restrict students or necessary to chat from happening during the online class.

Lock Meeting

Zoom has introduced us to this new feature, where you can lock your meeting after all the participants entered it, to avoid any unwanted participant or encounter.

File Sharing

Participants share or receive files, docs, pictures, PPT, take screenshots during the online session.

Test Meeting

Zoom allows you to Test session. You can analyze the functioning of your conference- internet stability, video, audio, etc., that how it works. By following these few simple steps;

- Launch the Zoom Meeting Test page.
- It will redirect to the Zoom app.
- Join the Zoom test meeting.
- Test the microphone.
- It will replay the audio for you.
- Set up an audio and speaker system for your Zoom session.
- Go onto the next test.
- Check how the breakout room and other features work.

Zoom itself is a self-explanatory application. With a little demo and hands-on experience, you will learn how to run this application easily.

Security with Zoom

Zoom is designed with a lot of protection options. It's an application that provides you with security and will protect your identity completely.

Here are some of its security features;

Email registration: It requires an email of attendees. And will show the host email address of every participant who signed up to join the session and can help you evaluate who's attending.

Use a gibberish meeting Name (ID): It's the best thing to generate a random ID for your meeting ID, so it can't be shared multiple times – with multiple people. Rather than giving your personal ID, this seems a better alternative. Did you know giving your personal ID is not advised because (first) it's no 'right' (safe) to share?

Plus, that's basically an ongoing meeting, and it is always running.

Secure your classroom: It gives you the option to "lock the meeting," and so prevents unauthorized and random or unwanted people from joining the session without your consent.

Password Protected: Your session can be password protected. By simply creating a password for entering a meeting session! Share with the required participant, so only those intended to join can have access to your meeting room.

Allow only known users to join: If you check this box, it means 'only' special members of your (interest) could join in. Otherwise, the app will not allow others.

Disable joining before host: You can also push 'Disable' to decline other members to join your Zoom meeting. This can happen before the host joins. In this case, a pop-up appears that mentions, "The meeting is waiting for the host to join."

Use annotations: You and your participants can also use annotations. It is available on the screen sharing controls. It prevents students from annotating unnecessarily when a screen is shared to disrupt a class.

Don't allow video: Teachers can also turn off a member's video. This can help block unwanted content or inappropriate discussion topic during an e-class.

Muting Others: While you cannot mute a student in a real-time classroom. Zoom allows you to mute them online. You can either mute or unmute a student/s. Most interestingly, you can mute the whole classroom too!

In the settings, there is also a 'Mute Upon Entry' available. This can keep the class hullabaloo at bay when your students go out-of-control.

Student on-hold: It is an alternative to removing/deleting a participant. This feature allows you to momentarily disable someone (like their audio/video for some time). If you want to do so, just hit on their video thumbnail. Choose now 'Start Attendee On-Hold' and activate it.

6. DO'S AND DON'TS OF USING ZOOM AT SCHOOLS, COLLEGES & UNIVERSITIES

In this fast-paced 21st world where technological advancements take place within minutes, everyone uses smartphones and other devices of this type.

Some years ago, there was no concept of mobile phones and computers. But now, we cannot even imagine having no phone with us – our world looks incomplete without them, right?

People are using mobile phones and computers for their professional and personal use both.

One of the latest uses of mobiles and computers is video calling. People are using video calling features for different purposes. There are several benefits of video calling with the help of the internet. It has made people's life easier than ever before.

Suppose we talk about the corona pandemic period, then we all have seen that almost every university and college started taking online classes with the help of video calling. One of the most used apps of video calling, which gained so much popularity, is Zoom!

This is one of the most favorite apps when it comes to video calling. One of the greatest advantages of video calling is that you can also switch to conference calling to start quick meetings anywhere anytime in the world; all you need is an internet connection.

Zoom has gained most of its popularity because of universities, schools, and colleges because teachers are using it to take online classes to stay connected with their students.

The Zoom user rate is increasing every day. With this quickly increasing ratio, many issues can also occur like security breaches, hacking incidents, and so on.

There are some security measures to be taken to keep your meetings secure and to avoid any interruption. Below we have mentioned all of them in detail.

Students are using a Zoom app to take online classes as we all know, educational institutes, universities, and colleges were closed due to the spread of the Coronavirus recently. Students can simply download the Zoom app from the Google play store. Zoom app can be downloaded on the smartphone, laptop, or I pad.

Zoom app can be used for various purposes in the educational institutes.

The Do's of Zoom

- Meet with group members for projects and assignments

University students get a lot of assignments and projects, and they cannot do it alone they have to discuss the project with other group members and take their opinion. Zoom is a very good app that can help you so that you can easily start a meeting and add all the group members in it.

The video quality and the audio quality of this app are very good, so you can easily talk and discuss the project with all your group members.

- Work on homework with classmates

School students get a lot of homework, and sometimes they cannot do it alone, and they need the help of their classmates; with the help of Zoom, they can easily talk and discuss their homework with classmates. And it's very easy to start a meeting on Zoom that even school level students can understand and easily use it. Zoom is very easy to handle application.

- Schedule online tutoring

A lot of students need extra attention, so they hire tutors who can come to their home and help them in their studies. For some teachers or professors, home tuition is the source of their monthly income.

Due to COVID-19, it's not possible to go to someone's home and give them tuition, so Zoom is very helpful in this too. Students, as well as the teacher, can easily download the app and start a meeting its useful for both the student and the teacher, students can easily get help in their homework or assignments, and teachers can easily continue their teaching.

- Host a meeting for a class

With the help of a Zoom application, you can easily host a meeting for your pupil, friends, and class fellows. If you are in a club or school, you need to communicate with your club members about various problems. Use this app because it is easy, quick, and simple to use.

So you can easily do that too by creating a Zoom meeting and communicating with other members of the club or organization.

- Record a presentation

University students get a lot of presentations because it's necessary to build up their confidence. There is an option to record a meeting on a Zoom app. You can simply open the app, turn on the camera and microphone, and record a presentation, then send it to your teacher.

- Preparing for a Zoom Meeting

To prepare for a Zoom meeting, you must find a quiet place like a separate room without any unwanted noises so that you do not get disturbed while you are in a Zoom meeting.

You must make sure that your device is fully charged before starting a Zoom meeting, whether it's a phone, laptop, or I pad because it will cause a lot of problems if your device gets turned off during a meeting, you should make sure that you have a reliable internet connection and you can also test your internet speed by visiting Zoom's suggested third party bandwidth tester, you can also test your microphone.

- Mute yourself when you are not talking

This is one of the most important points to consider when you are having Zoom meetings. You need to be conscious if your microphone is opened or not when you are not talking. Just keep in mind that you have to mute when you end up talking. This will help the meeting not to be distracted by sounds behind you.

- Require a password for your meeting

Keeping yourself secure should always be the first preference, and you should take all measures to set yourself as secure as you can. One of the most recommended settings to add a security layer to your Zoom meeting is that people should require a password in accordance to join your meeting.

You can do this by scrolling to the 'Meeting password' and check the box. Now Zoom will generate a unique password automatically, and everyone who wanted to join your meeting room will have to put that password.

- Control host and participant video

If you are the host your first preference should always be switching both host and participants video to 'OFF.' This mode will be really helpful to prevent any interruption in the class by any student. We have seen many examples that if students are allowed to turn on the video, they do some unwanted things to grab people's attention towards them and create a disturbance.

- Check 'enable waiting room' setting

Whenever we talk about Zoom meetings, the first thing that comes into our mind is the risk of security. We have thoughts in our mind that some anonymous person will join and create a disturbance. But if you are searching for the solution for this, you have finally come to the right place.

You will see an option of 'enable waiting room' in meeting settings if you are the host. Just check this box and freely go through your meeting. After checking this option, only those users can join, which are allowed to join by yourself. Zoom will give you all of the control to you. So you can allow only those people you recognize.

- Control sharing screen

When a teacher likes to control the sharing screen, they can simply click on the 'up' arrow, next to the 'share screen' icon. This allows you to take full control over the sharing.

Now under this, you will see the option of 'who can share?' click on this and choose "the only host."

Now Zoom will give you full control over screen sharing, and only you will be able to share your screen. If any other person wants to create disturbance and wants to share his screen, he will not succeed. This will add a security layer to your Zoom meeting, and you will feel more comfortable.

- Consider locking the session

Locking the session will prevent to enter any user after locking it. It acts as a door. When you have all participants that you need, then you can lock your meeting, and no one will be able to enter after that. In case if someone is dropped and needs to join you back, click on the unlock session for some time.

If you want to lock the session, click on 'Manage Participants" in the Zoom toolbar, then click on "More," and after clicking that, you will see 'Lock Meeting option.' Just click on this option, and you are good to go.

The Don'ts of using Zoom

1- Don't Use your Zoom meeting ID

Zoom is known for its security, and this is the reason because of which its users are in millions. Zoom has its default setting for you, which is most recommended. If you change them according to your requirements, you may face trouble.

One example of this is whenever you are going to take your class or going for a Zoom meeting, always scroll to Meeting ID and then click on Generate automatically. Now Zoom will create a unique Meeting ID and password for you, which you can send it forward to your class. Now make sure not to send your meeting room ID publicly. This will allow any anonymous user to enter in your room and can create a disturbance.

2- Don't use a Zoom chat feature while recording the session

When you are recording the session, and you are taking the class, you may have asked something personal, and your participants sometimes share their data in chat. This is completely insecure, and you don't even know where these recordings can go. If these recordings went to the wrong hands, there are bright chances of your audience will get scammed.

3- Do not use Zoom file-sharing or storage facilities

Students and their teachers sometimes use the Zoom application for file sharing and storage facilities. Recent studies revealed that Zoom is completely insecure for sharing files or if you are using it for storage purposes.

There are many best alternatives you can use other than Zoom for file sharing. One of the most popular and secure platforms for sharing documents and media is office365. You can use it for sharing with one drive, or its built-in sharing functionality is also one of the most secure ones.

4- Don't check 'enable join before host' setting

This is one of the most recommended settings while using Zoom to keep your meetings secure and on track. You have to make sure that this setting in the 'Meeting option' is set blank. This setting will keep your participants on hold, and they will have to wait until you join. If you enable this option, you will start facing trouble even before starting the meeting in the meeting room.

5- Don't enable screen sharing unless necessary

We have seen many distractions when there is no privacy enabled of screen sharing. For education, related users, Zoom sharing settings are defaulted, which allows only the meeting host to share his or her screen.

This helps keep away your participants to be able to share unwanted things in your meeting room. On the other hand, if you want to allow your participants to share their content, you can do this by adjusting settings on the Zoom app.

6- Do not try to manage a large session alone

This is a known fact that we cannot handle all things alone, but we need some assistance to make work smooth and to put you on track. When it comes to 'Zoom' meetings, sometimes, we have large sessions with university students.

At this time, you need some co-hosts which can assist you in making your meetings successful. They will help you to manage chats and have an eye on everything, and to act on time if something is going out of your control.

7- Do not allow students if they want to mute or not

This is one of the most recommended settings if you are taking the class as a teacher on Zoom with your university, school, or college students. We have seen students create a lot of disturbance when their microphone is not muted.

Sometimes they don't even know that their microphone is open, and it causes problems in the meeting. Zoom allows the host to set settings and have full control over all students' microphones. So with this functionality, only that student can speak whom you will allow talking.

8- Don't start Zoom meeting as a host if you have a slow internet

If you are a host, you need to know that your internet connection should be fast. This will be helpful for all of your participants. If you are hosting your meeting with a slow internet connection, this may cause your participants distracted.

9- Don't choose a noisy environment. Don't be late

The biggest issue of video calling is the noise in the background. IF you are a host or your microphone is opened, and you are talking about something, you must be aware of your surroundings. It should be a quiet place, so all the other participants should not face any disturbance.

10- Don't be late

This is one of the most important points to always keep in mind when you are a host that you have to be on time. This is because all of your participants are just waiting for one person, and it's you.

If you are not on time, then at the next meeting, no one will be at the meeting at the time you will ask them to join. So you have to consider this if you will be punctual, all of your participants will also be trying their best to be punctual.

11- Don't ask to question all in one time

Zoom is loved by many teachers and other professionals because of its useful features. When it comes to question-answer sessions, the most helpful feature of Zoom is 'Raise hand.'

This feature allows the teacher to ask students who are interested in asking a question can raise a hand. The teacher will be watching on his screen all those students who have raised their hands. There will be hand gestures in front of the names of those students.

If you ask the students to question all at one time, there will be a lot of disturbance, and you will not figure our actual questions to be answered.

Conclusion

Everything has benefits and some disadvantages too. It depends on us how we use it. We have discussed in detail about the Dos and Don'ts of using Zoom. We gathered these results after profound research, and you should consider all these points in accordance with having successful Zoom meetings.

By learning from these points, you will also be able to feel more secure by applying all these recommended settings. You should always be conscious when it comes to internet things because there is a lot of scams, and people got easily trapped who have less knowledge.

7. HOW TO CHECK HOMEWORK AND ASSIGNMENTS THROUGH ZOOM

After the coronavirus pandemic, Zoom has become the most popular video calling platform. The main reason behind its popularity is that almost all colleges, schools, and universities gave first preference to it and started taking their online classes on Zoom.

In the start, students and teachers faced some difficulties regarding privacy and security, but later on, Zoom managed to help both teachers and students and updated their platform according to the latest trends.

Why do Institutes choose to Zoom?

No need to buy a Premium plan

One of the greatest advantages of using Zoom is that you can access it free of cost, and without buying any premium package, you can have a meeting in which you can add 100 participants. This limit is enough for a class, that's why all universities prefer Zoom.

High Security

Zoom has improved their security, and now if you are a teacher, so as a host of Zoom meetings, you will be given full control. By applying privacy settings, no one will be able to enter your meeting without your permission.

On the other hand, you can also kick someone from the class whenever required. You can mute all the microphones of the class so no one can create a disturbance. You can do many more things to tighten the security of your Zoom meeting.

You can use Zoom for attending your meetings from anywhere anytime in the world; meanwhile, you can also check homework and assignments on Zoom.

Along with many other useful features, as a teacher, you can also assign assignments or homework to the students while using Zoom. The students will have to complete those assignments in your mentioned deadline, and you can mark them on Zoom.

First of all, you have to add an assignment to the Zoom.

You can do this by going to the assignments tool in the Zoom. You can select this by moving into the Tool menu. Now you will see the add button when you click on the Assignments tool. Here you can add your assignment easily. If there is no assignment added, it will show a message that there are currently no assignments at this location.

Title Name

Now when you click on Add, you have to give the name to your assignment as a title name. Your title should be unique and descriptive, so students can easily understand it when they come to see their assignment.

Now the third step is to specify the availability

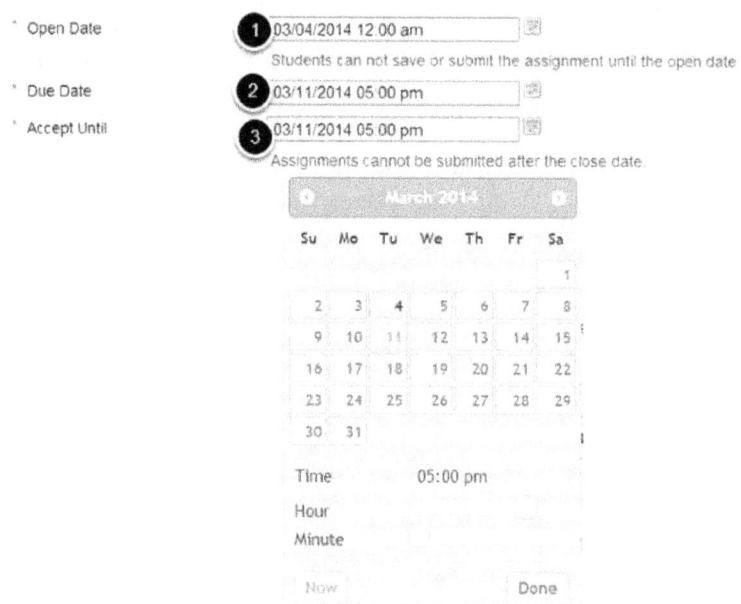

When you have created your assignment, the open date will show up as a default date, which will be the current date. You can set up these dates according to your requirements.

Open Date

This refers to the date when this assignment you are adding will go live and will be available for the students to work on it and submit their work accordingly. You can add whatever data you want.

Due Date

Due Date is simply the deadline for the assignment or the task you have entered.

Accept Until

Accept until is the date after the due date. This date allows students to submit their assignments even after passing the due date. Now, these late submissions will be marked as late. If you don't want to permit students for late submissions, you can set the 'Due Date' and 'Accept Until' date the same.

Now choose the submission format

* Student Submissions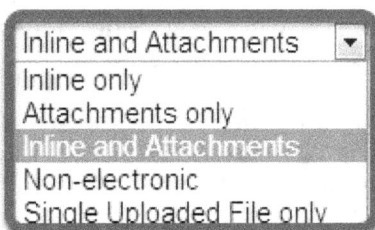

Zoom has given many submission formats, and you can choose any of them to accept assignments.

Inline and attachments

This is the default format chosen by Zoom, and this helps students to enter their work in rich text editor inline, or they can also attach the file, or they have the option to choose any of them.

Inline only

If you enable this option, you forbade your students to upload their attachments. This way, they are left with only one option – they can only submit their work in a rich text editor.

It is a highly useful thing. Using this, you do not need to download any assignment by any student – and grade all the work online.

Attachments Only

As the name suggests, when you have selected this option, students will have their attachments option enabled, and rich text editor cannot be accessed.

Single uploaded file only

If you want your students to upload a single file, only, you can select this option. Now students will not be able to send more than one file. All the other options mentioned above allow students to send more than one file at a time.

Allow resubmission (optional)

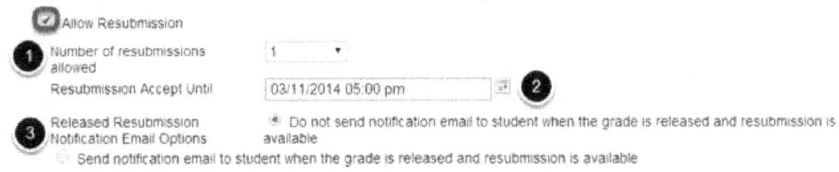

Zoom has given the freedom to the teacher whether he or she is interested in resubmissions or not. If you are interested, you can check the box of Allow Resubmissions and if you are not, just leave it unchecked.

If you are going to check this box, then you have to specify:

- The total number of resubmission for the students
- Also, mention the deadline for the resubmission
- You can also enable the email notification option for students to notify them when the grade is released, and resubmission is available.

Choose the grade scale

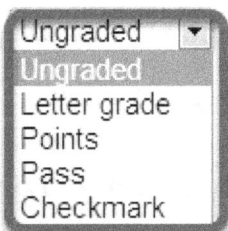

Zoom allows you to choose several grade options:

- Ungraded

This is a default option set up by the Zoom. This will enable you to collect students to work electronically but does not allow for grading in Sakai.

- Letter Grade

You select this option if you are interested in grading by letter only.

- Points

As the name indicates, by enabling this option, you will assign points to the assignments.

- Pass

This helps students to see if their assignments have passed or failed.

- Checkmark

This is a really helpful option for the teachers, which helps to mark assignments with a checkmark for completion.

Enter Maximum Points

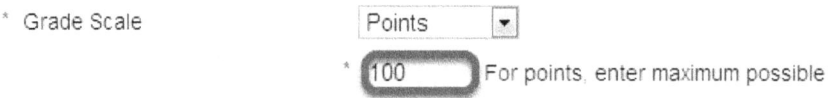

If you have selected points as your grade scale, you will have to set maximum points for the assignment which students may get.

Add Assignment instructions

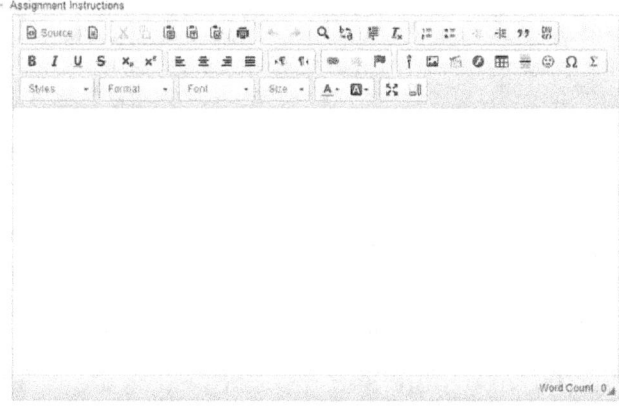

In the end, you can also add instructions for completing the assigned task or assignment. This will be helpful for the students to understand the nature of the assignment and also a better understanding to remain on the track.

Conclusion

You have seen how easy it is for teachers to assign homework or assignments to their students and also check them through Zoom from the comfort of their home. Zoom have made teachers and students life much easier, and they can have a physical feeling of a class even if they are taking their classes online.

8. ZOOM FAQS FOR TEACHERS

From where do I download the latest version of Zoom?

You can download the latest version of Zoom from the app store and the Zoom website or its download center. It is easy for teachers to find the Zoom as it is available at a Zoom website and stores.

How long it will take to download Zoom?

Zoom is not a big file that will take time to download. It will be downloaded within minutes, depending on your Internet.

What equipment do teachers need for Zoom?

To use the Zoom app, you need a device that can run the Zoom app. It can be a laptop, smartphone, pc, or tablet. Internet connection as it will not work without it. The teachers also need to have speakers and microphones as they have to teach the students. Speaking and listening to these two are required.

How much storage space does Zoom need?

Depending on the device you are using, if you are using an Android phone, then it will need 24mb to download on your device, and for pc, it will take little more memory. It will not take much space of your device.

Do we need an account to use the Zoom?

Yes, teachers need a Zoom account to use it. They have to create the meeting to send it to students so that they can join, but if they only want to join the meeting, they can join it without having a Zoom account.

How to create a Zoom account?

After downloading the app, you have to sign up to use it. The teacher or student has to enter the few details about themselves and then create a password. When you create the account, you can then use the on other devices by simply log in, enter username and password; then you can use the Zoom on any device.

Is the Zoom app free?

The basic Zoom is free of cost; you can use it as long as you want. You can also buy it to access maximum features. The big institutions usually buy it to maximum features; they have a license of Zoom. The teacher of such institutions has more access to use this app.

How many participants can join?

If a teacher has a class of 200 students, he can use the Zoom app to teach the class. The Zoom can allow a maximum of 300 participants in one meeting.

Is there a training session or guidelines to use this app?

The Zoom provides the live training sessions every week for teachers and students to learn how to use the Zoom app. It's very helpful for teachers. They can ask questions about Zoom in this weekly training. Every teacher should learn from this training to teach their students in a better way.

How a teacher can teach his students to use Zoom?

Teachers can guide their students by giving a quick intro about Zoom. Telling them to Visit the Zoom website and take live training. They can also help them set their own guidelines for a class when to hand raise, mute or unmute, and note-taking.

Do students need to create a Zoom account to join the class?

No, students do not need an account to join the meeting. They can join the class from anywhere without having an account.

Why teachers should use Zoom through canvas?

The Zoom meeting through canvas allows teachers to set schedules or calendars. It allows virtual class sessions and attendance reports.

How to create a meeting?

To create a meeting, you must log in to your account. After logging in, touch on the icon new meeting to create a meeting, then set the meeting options to start it, or you can also schedule the meeting by touching the schedule; teachers can set there class name, time duration, and password. It is a more secure meeting.

How to invite students to the class meeting?

When you create a meeting, you can then share its link with your students. You can also paste the link to any platform to invite your students; teachers can text the link or mail it - it is their decision.

Can I use my meeting ID to create a meeting?

Yea, you can use your meeting Id to create a meeting. Most of the teachers use their ID to create a meeting; they only need that to create a meeting.

How do I schedule a meeting in the future?

Teachers can schedule the meeting for the future by using the schedule option. You can schedule this meeting to send it to your students so that they are known for that meeting. You can set time and date for that meeting, the password for students to join the meeting. It is just like creating a simple schedule meeting.

How can students join a meeting?

They can join the meeting by clicking on the link that the host provides them. The link is direct access to join the meeting. You can also join by using your meeting ID; you will have to enter the meeting password to join it, which your teacher will provide you.

Can we get the Zoom plugin /add-on for Microsoft Outlook?

For Outlook users, access the Zoom plug-in by requesting temporary admin rights for your desktop through email or phone call.

Can you create a meeting of students more than 300?

Teachers can take the Zoom class up to 300 students bur if they want to take a class of more students than 300, then they have to apply the add-on license to a Zoom user account to take a class.

Who can edit the Zoom meeting details?

Zoom meeting details can be edited by only the person who creates the meeting (like the host). This person has access to edit the meeting. The teacher who creates the meeting can edit its time and date or password.

How to take class attendance in Zoom?

You can take attendance of students using Zoom as Zoom keeps the record of students when they enter and leave the meeting. It's available in a Zoom meeting through the canvas. You can go to the course and click the previous meeting and check the report; there you can see the students who have been in the class.

What do I need if I'm using Zoom outside of Canvas?

When you use the Zoom outside of the canvas, then you have to manually send the link to your students. It does not include the Zoom tab of the canvas. It works well but with fewer features.

Can I use a Bluetooth headset?

Yes, we can use the Bluetooth headset as long as they work and if they are compatible with the device.

How to connect the audio on Zoom?

We can connect the audio by just touching join the audio. It allows us to speak and hear.

Can you mute or unmute your participants?

Yes, you can mute and unmute the participants. Usually, it happens that some of the students left their microphone to unmute, and the background voices make a lot of disturbance.

So, you can mute it by turning it off, or sometimes they are creating a disturbance and are misbehaving, so you have an option to mute it. You can go to participants, and participants' names are shown with an option of mute and unmute.

How to take notes while taking a Zoom class?

You can take notes during a class; there is two way to take the notes when you are living in class.

Use a keyword command to switch between the tasks. On Windows, pc presses the alt + tab to switch between the note and the Zoom screen.

On a mac device, you have to use the command + tab key.

You can situate the note-taking application one side of the screen, and the Zoom talk window on the other. On your PC screen or laptop, you can position the Zoom window aside from the screen and position a note-taking application on the opposite side. Along these lines, you can see both applications simultaneously and effectively click to and fro between the two.

If a class has students more than 40 or 60, can I be able to see them simultaneously?

No, this is not possible. On one page, you can only see a maximum number of 49 attendees/ students; to look at other students, you have to scroll down to the next page. You can use two display screens or monitor, but it will be difficult to see them all at once.

Can participant change other participants setting?

No, they cannot do that. The teacher has the control to do that, which are also limited settings. They can only do that if they are the host.

Can we teach on Zoom without turning on the camera?

Yes, you can teach your students without sharing the camera. You can share the screen to teach them.

Can we share documents on Zoom?

Yes, we can share documents on the Zoom screen. Teachers do need to share the documents and slides to teach the students. They can understand the lecture better when teachers share slides.

Can we share photos and videos?

Yes, we can share photos on the screen. We can also share the video on the screen. The screen provides this facility to us.

Can we share the URL on Zoom?

Yes, the Zoom provides this option to share the URL. We can share the link of websites and other things.

Can we write on the Zoom screen or page?

Yes, we can write on the screen. It provides the whiteboard to share it on the screen. We can write about it and can explain the topic to students. Especially for math teachers, its very beneficial for them; they need this option to write and explain the problem.

How to share the screen on the Zoom?

To share your mobile or PC screen with other participants, you need to click the share option; then, you will see several options there, so you will select the screen sharing to share it with your students.

How to share screens from the second camera?

Zoom provides the alternative to use the second device to share your PC screen. You need to click on the share screen then tab on the advanced settings to access the two camera screen sharing option. After clicking the two camera options, your screen will be shared with other participants.

If you are using a Mac device, you can do this by clicking the screen mirroring button!

How can we share our Zoom window and toolbar?

We can share it by configuring the Zoom app and the browser. You can set both by clicking on the settings.

What annotation tool can teachers use?

Teachers can use all the tools that are provided by Zoom. Zoom provides the pen, pointer, erase, undo, redo, and color tool. We can also delete what we draw or write when we are done.

Can students become a host?

Yes, students can also become the host. Only the host can make students host. The teachers can transfer the control to any student. They can click on the student page and make them host by clicking on the host option.

Can we make co-host?

Yes, it can make the co-host by clicking on the managing participant. Chose the participant and click on make co-host. You can easily make any student a co-host.

Who can raise a hand in Zoom?

All the participants can use that feature. They use this option to ask questions when teachers see the hand raise on the screen; they know the student has a question.

Can students share the screen without becoming a host?

Yes, they can share the screen without becoming a host. They simply have to click on the share button and chose the screen sharing option to share their screen on Zoom. All the participants can see their screen also the host.

What else can students share on Zoom without becoming a host?

They can also share the whiteboard and documents on the screen. The students can also share photos and videos. You don't need the presenter to do a presentation.

How to record my lectures on Zoom?

You can record the lecture you gave to your students by just clicking on the record button; when you complete your lecture, click on stop to stop it, then click yes to save the recording.

Can students record the Zoom meeting on the cloud?

Students can record the meeting only locally. They cannot access the cloud to record.

How much space is need for a one-hour recording?

Depending on the recording type, if we screen record it, then it will take about 20mb to 30mb, and if we video record it, then it will take about 200mb.

Why I don't have a record button on the control option?

It is because your screen is not maximized. It's not enough to show all icons on the control option, or it may be your app that needs to be updated. If you have not enabled the recording, then do this from setting.

Can students chat with teachers?

Yes, students can chat with teachers during the meeting. They can text the teacher, and the teachers can also text them.

Can participants chat with each other?

They can chat with each other they have the option to send messages to each other. They can text the message to a specific class friend or send it to everyone.

Can the host see the chat of participants?

If you send the message to everyone, then the host will see your texts, but if you send it to a person in private, then the host will not be able to see it.

Does the host have access to stop the private chat between the students?

Yes, the host can block the private text message. In this way, students can only send a text to the host.

Is it a host choice to let anyone enter the meeting?

Yes, only the host can allow any students to enter the meeting. When they try to join the meeting, the host lets them be in the waiting room. After seeing the request, the host let them enter the class.

Can the host be allowed to lock the meeting?

Only the host has access to lock the meeting. When the host locks the meeting, no one can enter it. It's for the security of the meeting.

How to use the breakout rooms?

The Zoom allows the teachers to split their students into two groups for discussion. You can set the breakout rooms by clicking the meeting button and then click the advanced options button to access the feature.

Can the host do the polling during the meeting?

Yes, a host can do the polls whenever he wants during the classroom.

How many questions can be asked on polls?

Only 25 polls are allowed in one meeting.

Are Q&A sessions only available on webinars?

Yes, it can only be used at webinars.

If a teacher only wants their students to see them when they are saying something, what should they do?

This option is also available. To enable this, you need to use the 'spotlight' function. You can turn on and off accordingly.

CONCLUSION

How long have you been familiar with the virtual meetings? It's like forever, right! Though online audio-video chat is not new now, people have been taking advantage of these facilities (features) for many years. However, the increase in the year 2020 has increased a lot.

Once these types of chats had been confined to business, pleasure purposes only – remember the Yahoo chat rooms and Conferences back in the 2000s? The new era has made audio-video conferencing a must for everyone – let alone businesses and companies.

Plus, the recent outbreak of the Coronavirus has made virtual interactions a household name for everyone. Schools and educational institutes are also teaching online through different apps.

One latest and the most amazing app is Zoom. This eBook contains detailed information on this app (right from scratch!). Hope you enjoyed it; Happy Zooming!

ore comprehensive and structured tools in the About tab so that students can figure out what they need. No excuses here!

STOCK MARKET INVESTING

FOR BEGINNERS

Learn how to Trade for a Living with Risk-Management Strategies. Invest in Options and Forex with "Trader-Psychology" techniques. Get your own Financial Freedom

MARK BROKER

© Copyright 2020 - All rights reserved.

The content contained within this book may not be reproduced, duplicated or transmitted without direct written permission from the author or the publisher.

Under no circumstances will any blame or legal responsibility be held against the publisher, or author, for any damages, reparation, or monetary loss due to the information contained within this book. Either directly or indirectly.

Legal Notice:

This book is copyright protected. This book is only for personal use. You cannot amend, distribute, sell, use, quote or paraphrase any part, or the content within this book, without the consent of the author or publisher.

Disclaimer Notice:

Please note the information contained within this document is for educational and entertainment purposes only. All effort has been executed to present accurate, up to date, and reliable, complete information. No warranties of any kind are declared or implied. Readers acknowledge that the author is not engaging in the rendering of legal, financial, medical or professional advice. The content within this book has been derived from various sources. Please consult a licensed professional before attempting any techniques outlined in this book.

By reading this document, the reader agrees that under no circumstances is the author responsible for any losses, direct or indirect, which are incurred as a result of the use of information contained within this document, including, but not limited to, — errors, omissions, or inaccuracies.

INTRODUCTION

Did you know how many companies are registered with NYSE (New York Stock Exchange) and how much has been invested overall?

Here is a rough estimate: According to recent data, more than 3,000 companies have been registered, while the overall investment in just one stock exchange (NYSE) is about $15 Trillian.

Think of the other stock exchanges…..

The value of the international stock exchange is said to be $80 Trillian, Big Money – yeah – that means bigger gains…if you are in the game and (can play it correctly).

Now the question is how to learn it? Simple, follow the guidelines given in this comprehensive book, and you will be ready to play.

What's more interesting is 52 percent of Americans are Stock exchange investors. That shows how lucrative this market is.

So, before you start investing, read to learn the ABC of the stock market. It is written after doing research and is reviewed by some of the most successful investors.

Hope you would like this effort and enjoy reading and applying the strategies given in this book. In the end, if you ask me what that one thing that I should tell you as an expert to keep in mind (before beginning) is – it is: always remember: "a good Investment is always boring!"

> *"If investing is entertaining, if you're having fun, you're probably not making any money. Good investing is boring."*
>
> – George Soros

1. THE ABC OF STOCK MARKET

When we talk about investing in the stock market, we must understand that it is more than buying and selling shares. This activity can also be linked to other financial instruments where it is possible to operate in the short, medium, or long term.

The investment method used in the stock market is called "invest" if it is long term or "trading" if it is short.

Stock trading has become popular in this area of the stock market. This activity can be started online from anywhere in the world and consists of the sale and purchase of financial assets.

Trading consists of buying or selling an asset, then reselling or repurchasing it, and obtaining the respective profit. The advent of online trading has allowed many to invest in the stock market with little money, without owning large amounts of capital.

To manage the stock market, it is important to document yourself and study well the type of investment you are going to make.

What Is The Stock Market?

The stock exchange is an organization where transactions of different financial instruments are carried out through authorized intermediaries. This institution provides the facilities for its members, brokers, or operators to negotiate the purchase and sale of securities.

The stock exchange originates from the City of Bruges, Belgium, within the Van der Burson family of bankers. These organized meetings in his palace to make commercial operations or to transact assets, and they had like shield three bags of skin. Then in 1460 in Antwerp, Belgium, the first modern stock exchange arose, for years later, expanding to other countries.

Who Integrates It?

The stock market has been made up of companies, organizations, or public and private entities, which are the applicants for capital. Savers or investors who are the capital providers and intermediaries, brokers, brokerage houses, etc. also participate.

For companies to be able to list their securities on the stock market, they must publish their financial statements to determine their financial situation. When a company makes an offer on the stock market, anyone can know the information and performance of the company.

The stock exchange works like a large market or mall where stocks are bought and sold daily. Companies are listed on the stock exchange because it allows them to obtain new capital without having to borrow or borrow.

In this medium, any company can quote, as long as it meets the standards and the minimum investment requirements.

Role of the Stock Exchange

The time has come to show you what you want so much to know. Get ready to know the aim/mission of the stock market in any part of the world:

• Facilitate the transactions of the resources so that a better allocation of them is feasible.

• Support transactions by providing legal certainty.

• Guarantee liquidity, since assets such as shares and securities are converted into money.

• Inform truthfully and permanently concerning the values, operations, financial statements of companies, among other things.

• Contribute to the growth as well as the development of the capital and securities market.

• Organize the stock market through stock market operations.

How Does The Stock Market Work?

Below I will show you how the stock market works internally.

Undoubtedly, this is information that you must know before entering this wonderful and fluctuating financial world. Do you want to know them?

When a person has to buy or sell part of a company, he does it through the stock market.

If the company sells its shares for the first time, it makes a public offering known as the "primary market."

For a company to grow, it needs additional capital that requires the contribution of new partners.

Shares are issued to find these partners that are sold in the so-called public offering to those who are interested in investing. When a public offer is made in the stock market, the company is made public, and the interested party obtains the shares.

Subsequently, this shareholder can, in turn, sell his shares in the future if he decides, according to his convenience. In the same way that other investors buy it, they also evaluate the updated information of the company for their convenience.

Analyzing the information allows the feasibility of a good offer to change significantly from one day to another.

The purchase and sale price of shares is set by free-market laws, that is, supply and demand.

Those who buy set the purchase price and those who sell do the same; this is how operations are carried out, both actors setting their stance.

The shareholder always expects to earn periodic dividend earnings, or by selling his shares at a higher price. The holder is an investor who, by acquiring a bond, expects to generate regular interest or profits at the end of the term.

Stockbrokers are responsible for conducting transactions between sellers and buyers of shares. Investments in shares are considered variable income, while investments in debt as fixed income.

Can I Invest In The Stock Market From Home?

Here I tell you everything! Investing in the stock market may seem like a complicated task and only for large entrepreneurs, but in reality, anyone can do it. I only recommend that you study very well what it is and of course you go to the experts in the stock market.

Thanks to the internet, this market can be accessed more easily from home or mobile by different applications. However, just because it is easy to invest in the stock market online does not mean that it is easy to obtain earnings by shares.

Investing in the stock market online maintains the principle of buying and selling shares; it is done through online brokers. Benefits are obtained without the need to be in a specific place to operate the exchange, from where you are.

The online brokers will be the tool that will help us gain access to financial markets to invest in the stock market. You can invest in national securities and also in any company in the world, from small to large companies.

These so-called brokers can be obtained on web pages, applications, and other means such as banks (which allow investing from home).

The procedure is generally as follows:

• Open an account in a broker, the platform for trading your preference.

• You will obtain the corresponding username and password (if applicable).

• Each account will be associated with a bank account, where the money you will use for purchase and sales orders will be. The bank account will enter the money from the sale of shares, collection of dividends, and any other operation.

• Each operation will generate its commission, and you must bear in mind the brokerage costs, administrative expenses, and stock fees.

• Brokering costs are generally based on a percentage of what is invested for the services received. The costs or administration expenses depend on the country where you open your account; the commissions vary due to different factors.

Invest in the stock market: What platform to use?

There are many platforms to invest in the stock market. Below I will mention some of the most popular brokers or online trading platforms to invest or trade.

However, don't stop to decide! Take your time to try until you get the one that makes you feel safe and comfortable according to your needs.

How much money do I have to invest in the stock market?

You may have in mind that to invest in the stock market, you need to have a lot of money, but it is not.

I have good news for you, and it is that you do not need a lot of money, although I cannot give you a specific figure. Anyone can invest in the stock market on their own, without having as much money available to start.

When you invest more money in the stock market, it does not mean higher profitability; it is recommended to think in percentage terms, in terms of investment. You should start with little money to experiment, and then increase the investment according to the results obtained.

My primary recommendation is that you should save. That is, you need to have the ability to save to generate money, which you will then invest consecutively.

It is essential to make it clear that initially, your goal should be to gain experience and train. It is a complicated world, where many people end up losing a lot of money. It occurs because they do not form before fully entering the stock market investment.

You should also take into account the impact in terms of money that the associated commissions will have on your investment. Remember the commissions for a capital increase, custody of securities, purchase, and sale, collection of dividends, etc.

Can I start investing in a stock simulator?

A stock market simulator is a computer program with a very advanced interface that allows you to learn how to spend money in the stock market online. It has all the necessary tools to practice in real-time as if you were in the stock market.

It can support you as a fundamental tool to start trading in values and make some decisions without any risk! These simulators can be found in some specialized brokers or banks, and they are complex applications that are being commonly used.

Operating a simulator can avoid many headaches, helping you to train and learn, to have good knowledge. It enables you to get familiar with the interface handling play money, seeing the results of your decisions, to jump to reality.

"Unless you can watch your stock holding decline by 50% without becoming panic-stricken, you should not be in the stock market."

– Warren Buffett

2. THE MECHANICS OF OWNING, BUYING AND SELLING STOCKS

"If you aren't thinking about owning a stock for ten years, don't even think about owning it for ten minutes."

- Warren Buffett

The use of stock shares, whether it is getting dividends or speculating on their listing, is an increasingly popular and interesting practice. Of course, the risk of loss is also present, but depending on how you buy and sell your shares, this risk may be decreased. If you are wondering how to buy and sell stocks to large companies that are listed directly online, the following explanations may interest you.

Buy Shares to Become A Shareholder

A large part of individuals and institutions that buy securities do so to become a shareholder. It is the simplest use of stocks and their main objective. Indeed, when a company issues shares, it is possible to be a buyer directly online.

However, for shares already listed, this must go through an intermediary that can be an online agent or an online bank.

Of course, it is possible to buy shares directly from sellers who bought these shares themselves in the same way that you can resell your shares.

Buy and sell stocks with online brokers

People who wish to buy and sell shares on the stock exchange can do this from their homes. They can do so through an online trading platform proposed by a Forex broker. These Forex brokers make available to investors simplified trading tools called CFDs that allow speculation in the stock market.

These CFDs or Contracts for Difference allow you to buy a batch of shares on the stock exchange at a certain price and then sell it when the price has reached a level interesting enough to give you a profit on the difference.

However, the real advantage of CFDs for buying and selling shares on the stock exchange lies in the leverage effect, which allows you to multiply your investment by 100, 200, and sometimes even 400. In this way, you can generate significant benefits when operating lots of larger stocks over a short period.

For example, if Apple shares are at € 40 and you want to buy 100 lots, in theory, you would need an investment of € 4,000. However, if you use a lever effect of 1: 200 you can buy these 100 lots for just 200 euros.

Similarly, if this share goes to € 42 and you resell the lot of 100 shares, your profit will be 100 x 2, that is, 200 euros. It means that in a few minutes, you can double your investment.

Purchase and sale orders for shares

The Forex trading platforms that allow you to buy and sell shares on the stock market also allow you to enjoy practical tools to place your orders or program them in advance.

Thus, when scheduling a sell order for a certain price level, you no longer need to follow the market live, as your positions will automatically close at the right time. This method can be used to make profits, but also to limit losses with the "stop-loss" order that triggers the sale of your shares below a certain limit.

CFDs also allow positions to be taken directly for the sale of the securities, which means betting on the drop in prices.

When is it the best time to buy shares on the stock exchange?

Buying shares on the stock exchange can be an attractive investment, but it is not about buying any stock at any time. Indeed, the purchase of shares on the stock exchange is, first of all, a decision that must be made following a strategy. But then, when is it better to buy stocks?

When it comes to equity stocks, and to create a stock portfolio, it is preferable to buy the shares of long-listed companies to know in advance the potential of each security in terms of long dividends term. You can also choose to buy the shares of the innovative companies that issue their securities for the first time to be part of their success, although this is a bit riskier.

When it comes to online trading using CFDs, buying stocks is, first and foremost, a matter of finding the right time. Indeed, from a trading platform, you can access numerous international stock securities. But be careful: you should only buy a title if you think that your price will increase over time and in a more or less long term. In this way, you can obtain benefits by reselling the most expensive shares of what you have bought them.

Therefore, we advise you to buy shares on the stock exchange under the following conditions:

- the stock follows a strong and lasting bullish trend;
- a major event has just, or is going to, influence the share's upward price;
- technical indicators announce that the trend will remain bullish or a bullish reversal of a negative trend, and
- The sector of activity from which the share comes experiences strong growth.

When is it a good idea to sell the shares on the stock exchange?

Now we will be interested in cases of sale of shares on the stock exchange. A sale can be made to recover the money to invest it again or simply to pocket the profits if the corresponding title has increased in value.

Indeed, if you own some stocks in your stock portfolio whose dividends are becoming less interesting, it would be a good option to get rid of them to add more profitable stocks. You can also sell your shares to pocket profits because they have greatly increased in value since you purchased them.

When it comes to stocks trading on an online trading platform, things get a little complicated. Of course, you can re-sell the shares you have bought, but you can also directly sell a security without ever buying it. This method consists of investing in the price of these shares.

CFDs offer the possibility of investing both in the purchase and sale of shares on the stock exchange so that every opportunity can be taken advantage of even when the market is bearish. Thus, you can sell a share when:

- its price follows a strong and lasting downward trend;
- an event will take place or has taken place, and there is a good chance that it will lead to a fall or fall in the price of this asset;
- one or more technical indicators announce a sharp decline or bearish change for a stock, and
- the sector of activity from which the corresponding action comes suffers a major economic crisis.

How long do you have to hold stocks in a short-term strategy?

If you trade short term, or even concise term, you obviously will not hold your shares too long. A strategy like Day Trading, for example, will require the resale of your lots before the end of the session.

In this specific case, it is sensible to use a crowbar effect or bet a significant part of your capital to generate a substantial profit in just a few hours. Do not set yourself too ambitious a target, as you risk not being able to achieve it in time and suffering a bearish correction before leaving the platform you are speculating on.

If you trade for several days, you will only keep your shares until you reach a realistic target of a few max points. Consider setting a stop order in the right place so that your position closes on time.

How long do you have to keep stocks in a long-term strategy?

For more long-term strategies, it is necessary to take into account the possibilities of bearish reversals in the price of your shares. These micro-movements should not force their positions to close before reaching their goal.

In effect, you will have to use stop and limit orders at the same time. The latter must be established far enough from its opening price so that its position remains open in the event of a possible correction. You should also think about having enough capital in your trading account to be able to cover these types of cases.

When should the shares be resold?

Apart from achieving the goal that you have set, some particular cases will push you to sell your shares without waiting any longer.

For example, when the price of the stocks you are following passes below a critical point indicating a strong probability of decline, it is better not to wait and close your position so as not to risk losing more money. These levels can be determined by the levels of technical support observed in the charts.

Likewise, if you follow the economic news of a company whose shares it operates, some posts may create a risk, and sometimes it is preferable to sell your shares before they expire.

What shares can be purchased or sold online?

For some years now, the offer of Forex brokers regarding CFDs for stocks has increased considerably, and now many titles can be accessed from the trading platforms we have.

Of course, you will find Spanish, European and international stocks. All the actions proposed on these platforms are part of the large international stock indices. They are, therefore, especially popular, volatile thanks to precise strategies based on technical or fundamental data.

What stocks to invest in?

As you will no doubt have observed, the actions proposed by brokers on their trading platforms are very numerous and, therefore, it is becoming increasingly difficult to choose which assets to trade.

So what stocks should you invest in? Although investing in the stock market is not an exact science and it is not possible to foresee exactly which stocks will be profitable and which will be losers, it is sensible to analyze the sectors of activity that may experience strong growth.

3. WHO IS A BROKER & HOW TO CHOOSE ONE

Do you know what a stockbroker does? What are the main functions it performs? If you are not familiar with the answer to these questions, we invite you to read the following post, in which we will clarify everything about it.

Stockbroker: What is it?

The main task of a stockbroker is to advise other people who do not have sufficient experience to carry out operations in the diverse financial markets.

The stockbroker stands out for having good knowledge of finance and playing an active and main role in the stock market. It could be said that the stockbroker acts as an intermediary. It is the person who is between the broker and the investor who is interested in buying or selling.

The stockbroker guides and advises his clients in finance so that they can obtain the best possible returns. It is also in charge of managing the purchases, and the rest of the operations carried out by its clients. So it can be said that a broker's work cycle begins when one of his clients buys an asset and ends when he sells it and definitively closes the transaction.

Stockbroker: Functions

Among the functions performed by the stockbroker, we can find:

- Intervene in the purchase/sale of assets and the management of securities.
- It is placing of new securities in the market (Public sale offer, or also known as IPO). This refers to when a company is interested in starting to go public; it should be addressed to the broker, who will be in charge of finding a buyer for its shares.
- Inform and advise the client and companies.

Characteristics of a Stockbroker

We already know before that a stockbroker is the link between supply and demand in the stock market. Now, we will see the characteristics of the stockbroker and his trade:

- It is a commercial activity that can be carried out by any type of person.
- As it is an activity that anyone can exercise, not everyone can enter to carry out stock movements and transactions, because yes, no, it must go through the acceptance of a regulator. This process requires different requirements, including A minimum age, a specific level of education on the subject, accredit such knowledge if possible.

- The broker is under strict supervision at all times, promoting the good performance of the work without malicious news.

- The stock market regulator will constantly require the financial status of your account. Likewise, you are required to maintain a stable amount of equity.

- The agent will receive a commission according to the specifications of the agreement, this varies depending on the number of operations carried out, and may receive a fixed commission on their services, without the results of the operations affecting their heading, or, you can choose remuneration according to the percentage of their results.

How to choose the right stockbroker?

Investing is not as simple as buying and selling stocks, so the help of a professional is invaluable. A proficient stockbroker will devise a plan to grow your money while keeping your goals, risk tolerance, and time horizon in mind. Unfortunately, all stockbrokers are not created equal.

There are the bad, the good, and the ugly when it comes to investing. Choose the wrong broker, and it can cost you a lot of money on investment losses and unnecessary fees.

A Background Check Is a Must

You need your broker to be licensed and registered in the state in which you reside, yet you also want to ensure you have the right credentials, enough experience. And there are no major breaches of compliance.

All of that information is available by contacting your state's securities regulator. The American Association of Securities Administrators provides a list of contact information for state regulators here.

Equally important is how the professional is paid. Stockbrokers can be paid a percentage of their invested assets, an hourly rate, a fixed rate, or a commission on the shares they sell to them.

Unlike financial advisers who have a fiduciary duty to take into account the best interests of their clients, brokers cannot earn a commission on the sale of particular stocks, bonds, or mutual funds and can earn a commission. Often it is better to turn to a feed advisor or stockbroker who does not earn a commission. Because they do not receive paid commissions, they have no incentive to drive one action or investment idea over another.

Interviewing multiple runners is a must.

A lot of thinking and searching should be done to choose a doctor, and the same diligence must be applied to finding a stockbroker. It means in addition to checking your history; You must interview multiple brokers before making a decision. It is particularly important because you want to feel comfortable with the person who handles your money.

When interviewing potential brokers, there are some key questions to ask. First, know how the broker is paid and what he can expect to pay in fees. After that, you want to know how your agent will contact you and how often.

Nothing can sour a relationship faster than an unresponsive stockbroker, especially when you're uncomfortable with an investment or when the markets are trading. Each broker will offer different investment services and products, so you also want to know what their fees are charging you. For example, does the broker offer online tools to verify your accounts, communicate, and analyze your portfolio?

Also, does the firm give you access to property research and third-party research on individual stocks, different industries, and market analysis? If you're interested in real estate or international investments, you want to make sure that the agent you go with not only offers investments in those areas but is also well-trained to invest in those industries.

Check out these red flags.

The way your agent acts during the interview can tell you a lot about that person. The goal of investing is to achieve a goal that is unique to you. At the initial meeting, your broker should ask you about your goals, risk tolerance, and time horizon. But if he or she is advocating a specific investment idea or making guarantees on return instead, you should raise red flags.

If the broker doesn't take the time to know your goals and is only interested in telling you what they can do for you, it's a telltale sign that the broker has their interest in your heart, not yours.

Do your homework with references.

Often one of the finest ways to find a good stockbroker is through word of mouth. Ask your family, friends, coworkers, and other acquaintances that they use for their investment advice, and you should be able to get a list of some names.

A referral can be invaluable, especially when it comes to someone you trust, but don't take the recommendation blindly. You need to do your due diligence, which means checking the agent's background, uncovering the fee structure, and interviewing the person to ensure their personalities identify themselves. After all, many of the investors who were scammed by Bernie Madoff and his Ponzi scheme blindly invested on the recommendation of a friend.

The Bottom Line

Investing in the stock markets can be very complex and time-consuming and often requires the help of a professional. But while a stockbroker can provide invaluable service if your money grows, not all stockbrokers are created equal.

There are the good, the bad, and the ugly. Eliminating those falls on the investor and to do that requires a bit of homework. From consulting the agent's background to asking key questions before hiring someone, there are many steps to choosing the right agent for your particular financial situation.

4. HOW TO ASSESS RISK AND VOLATILITY

Assessing risk is a step by step process and is a basic part of the risk management of an organization. However, risk management is also conducted on behalf of an individual as there are several types of risks; hence multiple ways and purposes are served to conduct a risk assessment or risk analysis. Mainly, two types of risk are undertaken in a casual way, and that includes:

Individual risk assessment

Within individual cases and transactions, the risk is always involved. Risk can be assessed and analyzed in case of interaction between a physician and patient, a teacher and a student, a buyer and seller, and so on. It means whenever individuals interact with each other for any purpose. Individual risk can happen to occur between both sides.

However, individual risk assessment is affected by several factors like behavioral, psychological, ideological, religious, and others depend on the purpose of an individual's interaction with each other. Individual risk assessment affects rationally the whole process for which individuals interact with each other, and dealings and transactions are made among people.

So, there may be several requirements for individual risk assessment just depending on the nature of the task to be done by individuals, transactions to be made between them, and interaction is done among individuals. Whatever the purpose or reason for meeting individuals with each other, risk assessment and analysis becomes necessary to run the process smoothly.

Systematic risk assessment

Systems risk assessment or management can be seen in larger scenarios and broader sense. It can also be said an organizational risk assessment process that may require multiple problems, functional issues, and safety hurdles, etc.

Well, systems can be of two types like linear and non-linear. Whatever the type of system, several types of problems may occur over there, and it becomes essential to assess and analyze risks involved in each system. Risk can involve at all scales; from nuclear technology to food safety system and organizational or systems risks is evaluated on different parameters and requirements.

So, how to assess risk is another important point of our discussion, and the process of risk assessment involves identifying the amount of risk in a system. According to statistical and mathematical parameters, there are different ways to assess risk, and some of these are used commonly, but some are not used in routine life. Commonly used measurements of risk assessment include:

Standard Deviation

Standard deviation is a commonly used method for assessing and calculating risk; it measures the dispersion of data from its expected value. This particular method of assessing risk is used in the commercial industry, where investors have to make decisions about making investments or not. The current and expected rate of return is measured and compared for important decision making in the industry.

Beta

Beta is another one important tool to measure risk value in both individual and systems risk management processes. It is a mathematical and statistical term that is used to calculate the expected and current value of risk involved in any system or individual interaction. If a system has a beta value of more than 1, it would be considered the risk involved in the stock market.

Value at risk

The level and value of risk are analyzed with the help of this mathematical tool, and it is also commonly used in measuring risk in the stock market. The maximum potential loss of an organization is judged using this value at risk method, and important business decisions are made according to the results of the assessment of risk in the industry and stock market.

Conditional Value at risk

This is another important and commonly used way to calculate and assess risk in the industry and stock market. Basically, tail risk is assessed using this tool, and it is also helpful in understanding the current condition of the stock market and other industries.

Risk management and risk assessment are categorized in two ways; systematic risk assessment and unsystematic risk assessment. Systematic risk is assessing risk about the market, and it also affects the overall security of the market.

However, systematic risk assessment is considered unpredictable, but hedging can be helpful in mitigating the risk of the industry. For example, unfair political affairs can affect a large span of industry and stock market, and this can be said a systematic risk involved in the stock market and other related industries of a country. Put options technique is used to sort out this type of risk.

Unsystematic risk is all about risk is involved in a particular organization, company, or sector. This type of risk is diversifiable, and it can be mitigated by the asset diversification process. A particular stock, company, or industry can be affected by this type of risk.

What is Volatility?

Volatility is a particular mathematical and statistical term that is used in measuring the dispersion of a security system, a company's rate of return, and the stock market index. In most business and commercial cases, if the volatility is higher, the risk is also considered higher in the particular industry.

Multiple statistical tools are used to measure volatility in the commercial sector and the stock market. Volatility represents the current value of assets of an industry, and important business decisions are made, and strategies are formulated according to the recent condition of the company's finances.

Volatility is also referred to as the amount of risk that is involved in security and other systematic approaches of an organization. If the volatility of an organization is lower, it would be considered that the security value will not fluctuate at once.

Traders, analysts, and risk managers use different techniques and tools to measure and assess volatility in the stock market index position. Often high volatility is considered a sign of high risk involved in the business sector and stock market sector.

Trade and business become riskier if the measuring parameters show high volatility in the stock market index. Volatility is measured by commonly used statistical tools like standard deviation, Beta, and variance.

Standard deviation is a common statistical tool that is used to measure market volatility, and Bollinger Bands is used by traders and investors to make decisions and formulate strategies in the stock market.

Maximum drawdown is another one important tool to assess volatility in the stock market, and it is useful in calculating the index points in the stock market as well. Stock price volatility is also measured by the drawdown method of assessing risk and volatility.

A beta is also a common tool that is used to measure the stock market volatility and also helpful in determining the diversification and benefits of other assets of the industry and stock market.

Regardless of measuring tools for assessing volatility, it is also important to discuss the types of volatility in the stock market and other market sectors. There are two major types of volatility that go hand in hand in all market sectors and the stock market, and they include:

Implied Volatility

Implied volatility is known as projected volatility, and it is used to determine metrics of the stock market and other option traders. Having implied volatility, traders and investors are able to determine the right position of industry and stock market, and they can go ahead in all of their business dealings and transactions.

In this way, traders are also able to calculate the probability of the current stock market index and related trade and industry. However, implied volatility does not work in scientific affairs; hence there is not forecasting about how the market and industry will move forward in recent conditions.

Having implied volatility, traders cannot rely on the past performance of the organization and rate of return to move on in existing market conditions. They have to make estimates about the potential of the options in the stock market.

Historical Volatility

Historical volatility is also referred to as statistical volatility, and it gauges the fluctuations of security approaches after measuring and assessing price changes over. The rise in historical volatility means the price of a security will also move to the top than its normal range.

This is the time when traders and investors expect some unusual changes in the stock market and other market sectors. If historical volatility drops down, traders are not able to move on ahead in making decisions about business development or making any investment in the industry or stock market.

Whatever the types and categories of Volatility in the stock market, it can be assessed and measured by well-known statistical tools and approaches like standard deviation, co, efficient, Beta, and making a bell-shaped curve in diagrams of measuring volatility. Investors and traders use to compare different tools of measuring and assessing volatility, and it remains helpful for them to deal with different approaches to volatility.

Volatility and risk go hand in hand in all business sectors and stock market industries. If the volatility of the stock market is high, the risk is also higher, and if volatility goes down, then there is a low risk for making investments in the stock market.

Investors and traders need to have the most reliable and valuable tools for measuring and assessing volatility and risk involved in their business industry and the stock market. And remember a tip:

"I will tell you how to become rich. Close the doors. Be fearful when others are greedy. Be greedy when others are fearful."

– Warren Buffet

5. TOP INDICATORS OF A WINNING INVESTMENT

When it comes to stocks, people are always afraid of losing their money because of the lack of the right strategy. You can make your investment secure by applying different strategies. Some people try to learn about indicators of a winning investment, which helps them to grow their business.

If you follow the indicators in the right way and wisely, they will minimize the chances of loss and can help make more profit. These indicators are helpful for both long term and short term investment. All these indicators are present on stock market websites.

Some top indicators of a winning investment in the stock market are mentioned below:

Trend line

Type

Trend indicator

Computation

When three rising price bottoms are connected, they make an uptrend, and when three falling price bottoms are connected, they make a downtrend.

Signals

When stocks are showing above an uptrend, it means that the market is positive and bullish, but when stocks show below a downtrend, it indicates that the market is negative or bearish.

Takeaway

If you are planning for the investment, but when the market goes above, then the downtrend line. If you are looking for profit or avoiding the chances of loss, then sell when market prices go below the downtrend line.

Simple Moving Average

Type

Trend indicator

Computation

A simple moving average is simply the average fluctuation of the stock market in a selected period. Investors use this method for the long term and short term investment. People who set a plan to invest for the short term calculate average fluctuation for the last ten days.

Traders who plan for long term investment calculate average fluctuations in the stock market for the last 100 or sometimes more than 200 days.

Signals

If the stocks remain above than long term indicators in which investors applied a simple average method of 100 to 200 days, then the stock market is considered to be positive and bullish.

So it makes it easy for the traders to have a sense of making the right decision to invest at the right time.

Takeaway

When stocks approach long term moving average, then this is the perfect time to make your investment in the stock market, but when prices go below then moving average, then this is a time to sell. This technique is really helpful for making your money secure in stocks.

Rate of change

Type

Momentum indicator

Computation

When we talk about stocks, we must have to pay close attention to the rates which are changing with time. Rate of change is one of the best indicators which is used to check for the percentage change in prices in the selected period. Most commonly, traders use 14 days rate of change indicator, which helps them to understand better.

What it signals

After calculation, the positive rate of change indicates than the stock market is now positive, and prices are rising. The negative rate of change means the stock market is negative or prices are falling.

Takeaway

Fluctuation in the rate of change indicates that stock prices will make possibly turnaround. When prices are rising, but the rate of change is not affected, it indicates the reverse of trend.

Relative strength Index

Type

Momentum indicator

Computation

The relative strength index is based on the average ratio of high prices when stock rates rise. It also includes the average ratio of low prices when the stock market falls. This indicates how much a price can rise and fall on average. On the graph, it is plotted between 0 and 100.

What does it indicate?

You will have all the information about the relative strength index by Paying close attention to the graph. If the graph rises above then 70 to 80 it indicates that stocks are overbought. If the graph falls below 30 to 20, it signals that stocks are oversold.

Takeaway

Set up a plan to make the investment if the relative strength index goes above than 30 to 40 twice consecutively. Sell to make a profit or avoid loss when the relative strength index goes above than 70 to 80 twice consecutively.

Moving Average Convergence Divergence

Type

Trend and momentum indicator

Computation

Convergence Divergence is a difference between twelve and twenty-six-day moving average.

What does it indicate?

If you are searching for the best way to have an idea of an upward trend and downward trend in the stock market, then moving average convergence divergence indication can help you.

If the rate of moving average convergence divergence is increasing, then this indicates an upward trend. If it is falling, it indicates a downward trend.

Takeaway

Most commonly nine days, moving average convergence divergence is considered for buying and selling stocks. Make investment when it goes above than 9-day moving average and sell when moving average convergence divergence reaches below than nine days moving average.

Bollinger Bands

Type

Fluctuation, Trend, Momentum indicator

Computation

Bollinger bands indicator is composed of three lines. The first one is 20 days moving average second one is the upper band, and the third and last one is the lower band. The two bands upper and lower are plotted in such a way that they act as two standard deviations, and their core is moving average.

What did it indicate?

If you are interested to see the trend, it is indicated by the moving average. Now the gap between these two bands, which are upper and lower, signals the fluctuations in the stocks.

Takeaway

When prices start reaching the upper band during high fluctuation in the market shows stocks are overbought. On the other hand, when prices start decreasing or falling towards the lower band due to a high rate of fluctuation, this indicates that the counter is oversold.

Fibonacci Retracements

Type

Trend indicator

Computation

Percentages 23.6%, 38.2%, and 61.8% are considered the golden ratio in the stock market, which is based on the Fibonacci number series.

What did it indicate?

Whenever a fall occurs in stocks, most often stock market retraces stock prices to an extent before it happens to the beginning of the next trend. Many investors believe that these retracements occur almost close to the Fibonacci numbers golden ratio.

Takeaway

Occurring of retracement at 23.6% indicates the strong trend of upward retracement or downward retracement. Typically retracement ends on 38.2%. If the retracement goes over than 61.8%, this is the indication that the trend is over.

All about Technical Indicators

Some technical indicators are listed below:

Trend indicators

This is one of the most advanced techniques to grab an idea of market trends such as upward trend, downward trend, and sideways trend.

Momentum Indicators

When traders want an in-depth analysis of trends, momentum indicators help them out to have a better understanding of the market. They just act as warning signals. In some cases, they might be giving the right information. It does not mean that all reduction in market momentum will lead to the trend reversal.

Volatility Indicators

Understanding of fluctuation of stocks in the stock market is a goal of every person who has invested in stocks. Volatility indicators help to understand the unpredictability of the market. It is mostly measured in standard deviation.

Volume indicators

Volume indicators play a key role in making a decision, whether it is a perfect time for making the investment or otherwise. Small traders focus on this indicator because as soon people start selling volume decreases and rates also fall, then they consider it the best time for investment.

After some time people start buying once again and rates start rising, and they consider it the best time for selling with big profits.

On-Balance Volume

On-Balance volume is the most advanced technique used by professional and experienced traders. It is a more in-depth analysis of volume indicators. The on-Balance volumes gather all the information about the volume and setup all this information on a single-line indicator.

Now, this indicator adds up the volume on up days and also subtracts the volume, which is on down days. As a result, it assists in calculating the cumulative buying and pressure of selling.

It also tells us about the trends. The escalation in prices leads to the rising of On-Balance volume. Drop down in prices leads to the falling of On-Balance volume.

Average Directional Index

After knowing trends, it is most important to learn the concept of trend strength. Usually, it is graphed on a single line with the value ranging from 0 to 100. It is the most powerful technique which helps the investors to have a better understanding of a stronger zone.

Average Directional Index helps traders to build more confidence and aggressive position.

When the values on the graph reach above 20, it indicates the rise in the average directional index, and it represents that trend is getting stronger.

Relative Rotation Graph

This is one of the unique indicators which is used to visualize trends in the relative strength of even more than one or multiple securities against each other.

This helps to indicate relative outclass performers in the market and tell you to pay attention to the specific area of the market, which deserves the most. According to the most expert people in stocks, the relative rotation graph indicator helps to build a portfolio.

Final words

Indicators are simply the warning signals that give you certain information about different things, such as trend reversals. These can be used to have a deep understanding of the stock market. Before working on any indicator and going for the live trade, you just need to gather all the information related to that specific indicator.

Each of the indicators can be used in many different ways. Also, it can provide you with more in-depth information as long as you try to research it. It may be a tricky process for beginners who are just starting or have not started yet.

6. BASIC INVESTMENT TECHNIQUES

Investing a portion of your earnings is always a smart decision, especially in a world where nothing is permanent.

You never really know when you might end up needing your investments or savings. You don't always end up in need of them, but when you do, having a backup investment plan managed properly is a great way to sum up, your lifetime earning efforts. This way, when the hard time comes, you can be sure that you didn't work hard all your life to simply end up with nothing at all.

However, when you aren't very familiar with investment techniques, and you're more of a novice in this phase, you might end up investing your earnings in something useless or a waste of money.

Now to avoid such situations as a newbie in investing your earnings, its better you go through the basic techniques. This way, you can be sure that you'll end up investing your precious savings in something that's actually worth it.

You might think of looking for sources to help you learn these basic techniques, right? Well, you don't really have to go anywhere else, as we've got you covered with just the right basic techniques you'll need to start as a beginner in this. So let's not waste any more time and just go ahead to discover some such basic techniques.

10 Basic Investment Techniques for Beginners

1. Set a Goal

When you start investing your money, you need to firstly think of what you really want from your investment. This means that even if your basic motto is to earn money through your investment.

You should mainly determine what your income is along with your financial condition, how much you can really invest according to your circumstances, and how much profit you would need.

2. Early Investment is Beneficial

Yes, it is true, whether you're a college student or studying in high school, the sooner you consider investing in something that benefits you, the more it will get easier for you to invest with time.

This simply means that your earnings would increase over time, while the investments you make would also benefit you with the passage of time. Hence, with all these aspects, starting early would help you invest less money in the future and again more of the profit.

So it doesn't matter how less you can invest in the first place or what options you've got with the least of your savings or earnings; it's all going to benefit you over time. So just go for it as early as possible!

3. Invest a Constant Figure Automatically

Often we consider stalling and storing our money for some uses and needs, whether they're important or just something we're keen to invest in. And in such situations, we often utilize our investment money in such ways, ending up with no money to invest at all.

This gives the least motivation for investing further, and sooner when you'll notice, you'd probably forget about investing at all. But since it is really important for the upcoming time of your life, its better you go for an automatic investment option.

This way, the money you set aside for investing every month would be automatically taken from your account through brokerage service firms or automated investment services. Also, with this, if you even forget about the investment money, these services would make them don't.

4. Don't Invest Too Much

Now considering investing a great amount of your savings or earnings with the idea of having it doubled or profited into a figure that would leave you overwhelmed is good – and also something we all think of.

When you do start investing anything anywhere, it's important you snap yourself out of those fantasized dreams and get realistic.

This means that you can't go with investing a great number of your earnings without keeping your basic expenses in mind. Since you aren't sure of when the profit might arrive, and these bills are more of a constant paying need.

Hence, starting small with your investments, while calculating the money you'll need for your needs is certainly a great way to manage your earnings while also investing them.

5. Do Your Homework on Investment

Yes, we all need this, quite aware of everything basic when it comes to investment. But that's certainly not enough when you're getting ahead with choosing options and managing the dealing process on your own. Since this is more of official business, and you can't just act amateur and new in this, even when you are.

Hence, studying the basic terminology on making the right decisions and furthermore on stocks, bonds, funds, CDs, and other such investment options – is really important.

This way, you won't only learn about investment options and what suites you according to your position, but you'll also learn how you should deal with your investment and make decisions according to the market efficiency.

All this homework would certainly benefit you in the beginning, as well as for future investment needs.

6. Don't Pay High Commission

Remember this, when you go to professionals to help you look for investment options that would profit you well, you might end up being scammed by these professionals. This isn't something obvious, but as a newbie, you might end up facing these situations.

Hence, to avoid it, it's important you don't blindly trust professionals who would take a high commission from you for the investment options and further process.

In this way, you might end up paying a large commission to the professionals, while being rewarded with the least of profit afterward.

Hence, before you trust any professional and their commission demands blindly, its better you study on them and research on the investment options they offer you with. This would keep you safe from any kind of loss.

7. Don't Invest in One Place/Stock

Well, investing in stocks doesn't always result in large profits, but also leads you to equal losses. However, it's in your hands if you need to limit your losses and keep it all neutral.

For this, you can always look for investment options that are completely different from what you are already investing in.

This way, when one market ends up going down for a while, the other would be up. Hence, you won't just be left with loss only, but rather both profit and loss. This would be a way of diverse investment for you, keeping you benefitted with your investment at all times.

8. Invest in Long-term Options

This is highly beneficial, and that is why some of the top investors recommend beginners and everyone looking for basic investment techniques to always invest in long-term options. This mainly means that when you consider the short-term profits offered by a company and only do timely research on it, you might not end up gaining profits with that investment option for long.

So instead, investing in what might keep you happy and pleased for the next ten years, despite the ups and downs, are certainly the right company's you should look for. Hence, when you research on any company or investment option, make sure it is based on solid fundamentals as well as a strong and consistent long-term prospect.

9. Keep an Eye on Your Portfolio

Now before you start thinking what this basic technique is mainly referring to, let's get to the point here. So keeping a specific portfolio carried in terms of your investments is very good.

However, you can't always invest in the same place and never really go for a change. Because most of the time, we find options that are much better in the profit or the previous ones just don't profit us much anymore.

Hence, keeping track of your portfolio and changing your investment options every time the economic market changes would certainly be a smart move. This way, you can stay away from the investments that are giving you loss, even when they once offered you great profit.

And also, you can explore new options from time to time and make the most out of your money through these options.

10. Continue Research

As mentioned several times earlier, learning more on the economic market and what goes on in the present time is always a smart move in terms of investment.

This means that even when you've invested your money somewhere and have learned the most of that aspect and what's trending, you don't have to stop there.

But instead of that, reading and studying about the things you've invested in while also staying intact with the market trends every now and then, along with the global economic change – all would surely help you make smarter decisions in the future.

Final Words

Investments are the smart way everyone plans to save and benefit from their income nowadays. Whether you're someone old, a young entrepreneur, or just a student, you've surely come across multiple investment options several times in your life.

As much as it all seemed pleasing, beginners find investing their money anywhere a lot frightening too. A simple reason for that is the fact that they might end up losing their precious earnings or savings.

But even if you are new in something, it shouldn't be what stops you from taking a step forward. Instead, leaning the new ways of making more profit and the tons of options you've got today to invest in; is always a great way to spend your money as well as time.

Now that you've even got some basic techniques that can help you get started and going in your investment journey just righty, there' really nothing more you should be worrying about. So without having any second thoughts, just go ahead and apply these techniques for your better future!

Pro Tip:

"Patience is the key when you are investing in the stock market."

7. WHAT YOU SHOULD KNOW ABOUT TAXES

The stock market is a great place to pour in your savings as an investment. As only with some basic skills and knowledge on this market, you can make a great profit out of it. However, that's surely not all to what it is, as there are losses too.

But that's mainly what the stock market mainly revolves around; the losses and the profits. It's never really the same, and as much as you invest in it, the more you get to have a hold on this aspect.

However, learning just about the basics of what might result in a loss and what would profit you is not the only thing one should study. As when you're a beginner, you'd probably end up in situations that would ask you to understand more than just that.

Now, this can refer to a lot when it comes to learning everything about stock markets, but what I'm mainly referring to are the taxes.

Now whether you're a newbie in the stock market or someone who was around for a while now, learning the role of tax here is essential.

As only this way, you can be sure to make better investments in the right stocks; while understanding the tax criteria according to your position. So for a clearer view on everything about tax in the stock market, let's discuss some basics below.

The Long-term Capital Gains Rate Criteria

This tax rate is mainly applied to your profit, which is less in comparison to the rate that is applied to your other income that applies a tax. As an example, if your tax rate is 15%, you're most likely to pay a tax of 5% on your stock's profit.

Whereas, if you've got a tax rate of 25% to pay, then your profits tax rate would be 15%. However, this tax rate is mainly applied to the profit kept for a year or more, which is gained by the sale of your stock.

But that's not the tax rate applied to the profit from stock selling that is kept for less than a year. As instead, when you've got profit stored for less than a year, you're more likely to pay the tax rate for it, which is equal to the ordinary tax rate you pay on your income.

Reducing Tax on your Stock Sales

Here is a point to remember, when you determine the profit of your stock sale in a specific calculation method, you are more likely to understand the exact meaning of the variables in the formula. This mainly means that you can plan the exact amount in a way that you reduce the liability of the tax when you sell your stock.

Now, most of the time, we consider the full amount of the check received after selling stock to be the one that we should pay a tax on. However, that's certainly not the complete truth, as there are ways you can subtract the amount of tax you pay according to how much you can.

A simple formula to get this done is to subtract the basis of your tax amount to the sales you've received, and you'll get a deductible loss or a taxable profit you can eliminate from this profit of yours. This way, you won't really end up losing too much of the unexpected tax from your profit, especially when you don't even want to.

Now one might consider how they can really reduce the sales proceeds in all this calculation so that you don't pay too much tax, right?

Well, a simple and obvious way to do that is to pay some commission to a broker who would help you get through this. So instead of paying too much on the tax, you can pay a little in order to make sure you can get along with this formula of reducing your sales tax.

Next, is the basis in the formula just mentioned? Well, if you're still wondering what that might refer to, and then you can consider it to be the main cost of the stock you'll be selling. However, that's not all, as it can also include the dividends that you've reinvested in the stock or the commissions you pay to the opposition.

Yet, in some cases, if you've inherited a stock, then the basis would simply be determined as the fair market value of the stock after the date of the decedent's death. Also, if you've received the stock as a gift to you from someone, then you can consider the basis to be a lower amount of the fir-market value, according to its value, at the time the gift was sent to you.

Experimenting with the Wash Rule

Now you might have heard of this rule in the stock market, but understanding it from a closer perspective is also very important. Since we're mainly discussing taxes in the stock market, this rule also revolves around just that.

However, it's mainly the practice of selling a stock for profit when you're in the position of gaining loss from it, and when you do sell it and gain the profit, you buy it back instantly.

Now, this isn't really what the rule mainly is, but rather where you can apply it in your stock affairs. Hence, with the help of the 'wash rule,' you get to prevent the loss you'd get on the sale of a stock if you buy its replacement stock in the time period of 30 days.

This mainly helps you get out of the limitations applied by the IRS; that doesn't allow an investor to claim the loss after selling stock and then buying it again in less than 30 days. Hence, when you've got the 'wash rule,' you can make less loss through a stock.

Deduction of Capital Losses

When you face losses in your stock market, you are allowed to deduct an amount with respect to the losses from your tax returning amount. Now as much as this is a benefitting factor of the stock market, you're also supposed to face some limitation here.

This means that you are only allowed to gain a specific amount of your losses through the tax return every year. Hence, no matter how many stocks you sell at a loss, you are going to be able to deduct only $3,000 per year. And the rest of your loss would be taken forward to provide to you in the coming years.

However, if you're willing to first calculate all your losses and gains through this specific limitation and understanding how what you'll be ending up with, you can always apply the capital losses against the capital gains you achieve – both in the present year and the one's coming afterward.

Other Deductible Expenses in Investment

Often we don't pay attention to a specifically less tax deduction from our profits, which is mainly the commission of the brokers in the stock market. However, these aren't just any brokers, but rather the one's who either manage our mutual fund account or simply provide us with advisory services in the stock market. And so, this tax amount is deducted as a fee for their services offered to us.

But if you don't feel like allowing the deduction of this fee, then you've always got a long-term option of having these fees deducted back to your account. This deduction to provide your fees back to you can take place as an investment expense on Schedule A, which would be possible on your tax return.

Now in terms of understanding the exact amount deducted from your profit for the broker fees, you'll need to do a little work. This doesn't mean proper research and study on it, as most of the broker fees depend upon the 1099s of year-end statements – where you can find a statement provided on the total charged fee for a year.

But since many brokers do not follow this criterion, you might simply have to contact your broker and ask them for how much fee you paid. This way, you can have a clear idea of how much you would want to take back as the deduction.

Final verdict

Almost everyone nowadays considers the stock market as a great source of investment and profit income. And so, we'd quite often notice how most of the people around us are a part of this market. And why not? When there's such a huge stock market available for you to invest and gain profit from, there's hardly any reason one should step back from it.

However, even with all the pros on might consider this hugely benefiting market, there are certainly some loopholes one should consider before stepping into it. Now one obvious one here might be the fact that you might lose just as much as you would gain (unless you don't master the investing techniques). But other than that, the tax factor in the stock market is also something one should study about; before you end up noticing that your profits have lessened.

Now keeping that in mind and the fact that not many consider the taxing of their stocks to be as important of an enlightening subject for them as others in this aspect, we've aligned everything important you should learn about. Now keeping that in mind and the fact that not many consider the taxing of their stocks to be as important of an enlightening subject for them as others in this aspect; hence, just go ahead; and make the most of it!

8. ALL ABOUT THE BULL & BEAR MARKET

Incorporate the world; you must have heard the words Bull and Bear; this is a general description for dual market conditions rise and down. Simply, a bull market is just about the market is on the rise, and its economy is sound and stable, whereas a bear market describes the down condition of the economy in which stocks are in decline in value.

This particular name and the term is used to describe what markets are doing in general and what its positions in the current situation are. Bull and Bear also narrate about appreciation and depreciation of market value. Investors and traders are also given names as Bullish and Bearish according to the particular market conditions.

Bull and Bear both names are just phrases that indicate the current condition and situation of the market; hence behavior and mentality of investors and traders can also be judged in a particular scenario. If the market is Bull, the investors would be named as Bullish, but if the market is bear, then they would be called Bearish.

There is a historical background behind these particular terms and names of market conditions, and they are related to the psychology and gestures of both animals bear and bull. However, it is also said that actual expression for these terms is just unclear right now, but it can be described according to bull and bear's action.

For example, a bull is always seen to attack by its horns upwards while the bear is analyzed attacking swap its paws downwards. So these factors can be considered for giving names to market conditions; up and down.

Actions of both animals are related metaphorically to the market conditions. If the economy is up, it would be considered a bull market, and if the stock goes down, it would be named as a bear market.

Whatever the origin of these phrases and terms, they are interesting and seen to be rational in the corporate world. Our next discussion would be based on all about the bull and bear market. What market conditions and indicators can fall in both types of terms or categories? So, keep reading the following lines for the interesting narration of the bull and bear market.

Some of the usual indicators of the bull market include:

High Gross Domestic Products

This is simply a usual indicator for a well-established, stable, sound, and flourishes economy as it is bull market condition. In this particular condition, GDP remains high; hence consumer spending is also upward.

Rising Stock Prices

Rising stock prices leave a very good impact on the mentality and behavior of people associated with bull market conditions, and they get more confident in making investments in the industry. Prices and rates are also increased in this particular market condition.

Longer Stock Trading

The whole environment and climate of the market last cool and hopeful, so investors feel free to busy their shares on more business sides. This is the reason this condition is related to longer stock trading terms.

Lower Unemployment Rates

In bull market conditions, more and more people are hired on jobs, and there is no concept of unemployment. Up-gradation of business means there is growth in the workforce, and most of the people are hoping to be part of the good ear of industry.

Another good point of bull market conditions is that it remains longer than bear market conditions. Not only this, but the average total return for a bull market is also seen to grow. If we see a global scenario of bull market conditions, we can find notable examples of bull market conditions in the corporate world historically. Like:

The Bull Market History

The 1940s-1950s

It was a time after post second world war, and it was the bull market condition when the US economy was at the top, and most of the soldiers were returned to their homes.

1980s-2000s

This was also a golden period for US economic conditions, and it was a bull market when a 600% average return rate was determined to be gain in the overall corporate world.

Today

US economic conditions have consistently grown up since 2017. This is also said to be a golden era of the corporate world in the United States as jobs are always available over there, average returns for investment have grown up, investors are always ready to put their part in trading activities and business.

So this is a bull market in a nutshell; however, whatever the condition of the bull market is, it can exist with a bear market. Further, we are going to describe the same information about the bear market. So don't leave it without reading the following lines.

In contrast with the bull market, a bear market is just all about going down, getting pessimism, the condition of trade is stagnation, trends are down, people are unconfident and insecure, stocks are sold rather than buying, etc. This is a bear market condition where there are no jobs, no hope, no business planning at all.

The Bear Market Indicators

Some of the usual indicators for the bear market include:

Fall down of Market Prices

Investors and traders become bearish in a bear market, and they are not willing to buy a new share of the business that results in complete fall down in market prices and stability of industry as well.

Complete Unemployment

Unavailability of jobs or relatively low rates of employment is a clear sign of bear market. Fall down of companies and shareholders results in layoffs and downfall of the workforce as well.

Shorter Stock Trading

In the bear market, stock trading conditions get more bearish, and investors do not buy and sell stock shares. The industry stops at all.

Although a bear market is seen to be very bad, it does not last long at all. A study by Morningstar reveals the fact that average bear market conditions last just for 1.4 years in the history of the corporate world.

Regardless of indicators and facts about the bear market, there are several notable examples of the bear market that last in the history of the US economy.

The Bear Market History

1929s

During this session of the year, the US economy was seen to be paralyzed entirely as there were no jobs; people get homeless and lost wellbeing. Not only America but the entire world was impacted by the bear market conditions in the United States in 1929.

The 2000s

This was the time when there was a severe downfall of tech companies in the United States, and it was called a bear market.

2008s

2008 was the time for the housing market crash. This was a severe bear market as there were no jobs, homeowners lost their homes and traders get empty and fail to even think about investing in stock shares. This bad bear market is felt till now the United States has come into the bull market.

Investors and traders are always seen scary about the bear market as it is a scary and empty region in the corporate world, but it does not last long as we have seen in the previous history of the United States economic survey and information.

From our discussion put above, you can now better understand a clear difference between the Bull and Bear markets. Both conditions are contrary but go hand in hand with each other.

You know, up and downs are parts of life, and everyone has to go through both of these phases, whether it relates to the personal life of an individual or it is associated with a corporate world. We can say that the Bull and Bear market reflects the general overview and behavior of practical life.

Don't you think that this particular term or name of market conditions is pretty much interesting? These market conditions are associated with the attack actions of two animals Bull and Bear.

Well, the importance and existence of both the Bull and Bear market are undeniable, but both animals are remarkable for their incredible and unpredictable strength to attack and defense. Some facts reveal the evidence of Bull and Bear market concepts from the era of Elizabeth and ancient times when bull and bear were together to entertain the people come in the crowd.

The fight between Bull and Bear is famous in this regard, and this is the reason both market conditions are named accordingly.

So, what do bull and bear market means for you become important to ask after giving you solid facts and information about bull and bear market? Hopefully, this would be pretty much enough about the bull and bear market. Good Luck with your investment!

9. COMMON STOCK EXCHANGE TERMS AND WHAT THEY MEAN

If you are planning to start investing your money in the stock market, then there are some common stock exchange terms that you must know. These terms are very important in understanding the behavior of the stock market.

You should also have known the basics before diving onto the live trade. If you want to become a successful trader, these terms will assist you in achieving your goals and building your career in the stock market.

What is the Stock Market?

In short, any exchange allows people to buy and selling of stocks and give permission to companies to issue stocks to people. Stocks represent the company's ownership or equity. Shares are the units of the company. When people invest in the stock market, it means that they have bought shares of one or more than one stock.

What does the stock exchange term mean?

Stock exchange terms are slang specifically for industry security. Professionals and expert traders use these terms to talk about different game plans, patterns, charts, and many other related elements of the stock market industry.

Common stock exchange terms are listed below:

1-Annual Report

The annual report is specifically made by the company for its shareholders. This report is designed in such a way that it attracts the shareholders. The annual report carries all the information about the company's shares and their game plan for the present and future. When you are going through the annual report, you are gathering information about the company's financial situation.

2- Arbitrage

This is one of the most advanced terms in the stock market, which every trader should know. This refers to buying stocks at a low price from one market and selling at a higher rate on another market.

For example, sometimes a stock ABC trade on 50$ on one market and the same stock on the other market trade on 55$ so traders buy shares on low price points and sell them on higher rates to make the profit.

3-Averaging Down

When stock prices fall, and you plan to buy stocks on lower rates, your average buying prices decrease. This strategy is used most commonly in the stock market. After buying, you plan to sell those stocks shares when the stock market rebounds.

4- Bear Market

A bear market is opposite to Bull market. It means that the overall market is negative or falling. In this stage, the market falls up to 20% the quarter after quarter. This is one of the scariest situations for big investors because their investments are at great risk.

5- Bull Market

Bull Market is opposite to the bear market. Bull market meant the rising of the stock points. In this stage, people start investing money in the stock market because of their positive behavior.

6- Beta

This is the whole relationship between the stocks and the overall market. If stock ABC has a beta of 5.5, it means that for every one-point movement in the market, the stock ABC moves 5.5 points and vice versa.

7- Blue Chip Stocks

These are the stocks that large backup companies and leading industries. Blue-chip stocks are well known for their management and sound records. This expression is thought to be derived from casinos where blue gambling chips are used.

8- Bourse

In short, Bourse is a modern and more advanced name of the stock market. It means where people gather for the purchasing and selling of stock shares. Most commonly, it refers to Parris stock exchanges or non-US stock exchanges.

9- Broker

Many people who are beginners and don't understand the behavior of the stock market make contact with different brokers. These brokers are experienced traders who have sound knowledge of trading of stocks. These beginners contact these brokers and ask them to buy and sell stocks for them. Brokers charge high commissions for these services.

10- Bid

Bidding is as common and simple as we do in freelancing and other daily projects. In stock market bidder, who is a buyer bid for a specific share. Bid means the buyer willing to buy the share on his desired rates. The bid is made according to the asking price of the seller.

11- Close

Simply this refers to the time when trading will stop, and the stock market will close. Its timings vary from country to country. Each stock market has its own time of closing and opening. After closing the stock market, it is not available for live trade.

12- Day trading

This is one of the most advanced terms in the stock market. Day trading refers to buying and selling of stocks shares on the same day. This method is used by many experienced traders.

After buying shares, people wait for the next day to sell them at much higher rates. But there are 50/50 chances that they may end up with profit or loss. So, Day trading is a smart strategy, but it requires a lot of experience to make profits.

13- Dividend

Many companies offer incentives to attract more traders to their company. Some companies pay their shareholders one of their earnings portions, which are called the dividend. Some companies pay dividends annually or quarterly. Not all companies offer a dividend.

14- Exchange

Exchange refers to a place where thousands of investments are traded daily. There are many popular exchanges in the world. New York Stock Exchange is one of the most popular exchanges in the world, which is present in the United States of America.

15- Execution

We are familiar with this term in the sense of computer where it means the completion of a task. In the stock market, it also acts the same as in the said case. When a trader buys or sells stock shares, after completion, it is said that the transaction has been executed.

16- Haircut

The haircut is the most known term used in the stock market. It is the slight difference between the bid made by the buyer and the asking price of the seller.

17- High

High indicates the milestone reached by the stocks. It points out that the specific stock has never reached such a high price before. In the stock market, there is also one other high. This high is used to demonstrate the milestone reached by stocks in a specific period. It may be fortnightly or in 30 days.

18- Initial Public Offering

Initial Public Offering means that when a company decides to expand its business and offers its stocks available for the public. The Securities Exchange Commissions is responsible for issuing Initial Public offering and is very strict against its rules.

19- Leverage

Leverage is considered the riskiest and dangerous game tom plays in the stock market. After having your complete research, you decide to borrow shares from your broker and set up a plan to sell them on higher rates. If you successfully sell those shares on higher rates, you again return those borrowed shares to the broker and keep the difference.

20- Low

Low is opposite to high. It indicates that the specific stocks have never fallen to this price before. Low is also demonstrated for a specific period may be weekly or monthly.

21- Margin

Margin is almost the same as that of leverage. It is also considered one of the riskiest game. It is an account that allows you to borrow money from the broker to invest that money into the stocks. Now the difference between the loan which you borrowed from the broker and rates of the securities is called margin.

Margin is not for beginners; even the most experienced traders fail to apply this strategy.

22- Moving Average

Moving average is the average price of the stock shares at a specific time. 50 and 200 are considered the best common time frames to study the behavior of the moving average.

23- Open

Simply open refers to the time when the stock market is open for the live trade. Traders start buying and selling of stocks according to their plans. This varies from country to country. Every stock market has its own time to open and close.

24- Order

Order is the same as bid, but in the order, you decide to buy or sell stock shares according to your plan after deciding your order to sell or buy the stocks. For example, if you are willing to buy 200 shares, then you have to make an order.

25- pink sheet stocks

Many beginners take start with pink sheet stocks. If you are just planning to invest in this stock market, you most probably have listened to pink sheet stocks. These are penny stocks and are traded on a small scale, and each share price is 5$ or even less than that. Because these are the shares of smaller company's, you will not find them on the big markets such New York Stock Exchange.

26- Sector

There are dozens of companies that belong to the same industry. These companies are available publically on the stock market to buy their shares. These stocks groups which belong to the same industry are called sectors.

Many experienced traders trades in a single sector, such as cement or steel. There are many advantages to investing in the same sector because it is much easy to predict the fluctuations.

10. TIPS AND TRICKS FOR INVESTING IN THE STOCK EXCHANGE

Almost everyone is searching for a shortcut, which leads them to success. Its human nature, we always look for miracles that can change everything. When it comes to the stock market, people are scared of losing their investments. They find ways that could become beneficial for them to secure their investments and make a profit.

Avoiding loss in stocks is not an easy task, and even sometimes, experienced traders fail to achieve their goals. With time by learning more and more about stock market behavior is the only way to get success.

There are some pro tips and tricks for investing in stock exchange which every trader should know:

1- Invest in Index Fund

One of the most important tips for investing is to invest in an index fund instead of looking to invest in individual stocks. It also depends upon your goals, but investing in individual funds is not a good approach.

If you are taking stocks on a serious note, then investing in an index fund in a specific sector can be a great way to build your portfolio. It also helps to focus on one thing. There are some important points to remember while investing in an index fund. These are expense ratio and assets in total.

2- Focus on Mutual Funds

It is a well-known saying that putting all eggs in one basket is always the worst choice. When you are planning to buy some stocks shares, do remember not to invest in single stocks. Always find good growth mutual funds and put your money in it. This approach is the most secure one, but it seems boring and time taking. But many people love to focus on mutual funds. This technique helps to minimize the chances of losing investment.

3- Timing the Market

Many beginners think that there are sometimes when the selling or buying of stocks can make them profits. They all end up losing their money. Learning market volatility is not an easy task. Some experienced traders also believe that timing the market is not a good way to dominate in the stock market. You have to experience about market fluctuations and sell or buy stocks accordingly. There is no best and worst time to buy or sell stock shares.

4- Set Goals

Setting up goals is always the best method that every person should follow, which leads to success. People without goals are like blind people. Before diving into the stock market, first of all, you should set the goals of your investments. When you have set a long term plan, then you will have a better understanding of what to do and how to reach the destination.

5- Five Golden steps of trading to learn:

- **Setup:** A setup is composed of a high probability pattern to follow on the chart. It also ensures the reason why you are considering a trade. You need to track them to make sure that how consistent they are.

- **Strategy:** There must be a way to trade the setup and the perfect plan for it, which seems to be working. Beginners should always work on the strategies and spend time on it.

- **Entry:** Entry can make a big difference. If you enter the right way, then you will end up making a profit. On the other hand, the wrong entry will lead you to make run out of money.

- **Stop:** There should always be a stopping point when you are going through live trade. This whole thing should be pre-planned, and you should know why you are going to stop.

- **Profit Target:** When things start getting right in your favor, you sometimes make bad decisions. Instead of regretting later on, make decisions to set a profit target.

6- Have a balance of investments

There are three types of investments, which are low, high, and moderate risk investments. All these investments have some pros and cons. keeping a balance between these three risky investments can be a wise approach. If you are just starting, then prefer to invest in low-risk investments.

As soon as you get some experience, move to the moderate and then high-risk investments. Low-risk investments can make you small profits, but instead of losing all of your money in high-risk investments, consider low and moderate risk investments.

7- Think for long term

We always look for short term methods which can make big profits. But in reality, these things are nothing. So always plan for the long term. Try to invest your time in learning the behavior of the stocks to make more profits in the long run.

8- Buy value stocks

Value stocks mean stocks that are established with minimum variations. If you want to get success in the stock market, you need to learn the volatility of the stocks. Buying value stocks can make your investments much safer and secure. While looking for value stocks, consider their earning ration and price to sales ratio.

9- Diversify investments among sectors

No one can predict the stock market uncertainty. A sudden change in the country or even abroad can affect the stock market. This sudden change may be a political activity, a storm, a disaster, or any unusual thing. Diversification of investments among sectors is a proven way to minimize the chances of losing investments.

10- How much risk you can take?

Before start trading, you should make your mind clear that how much risk you can take. There are some pros and cons of this strategy. This strategy helps to have a better understanding of your game plan. Whether you are going for long term or you have made your plan for the long term in both cases, you need to be clear about how much risk you can bear.

11- Control your emotions

One of the key activities to achieve your goals in the stock market is to be patient. The stock market is considered one of the most uncertain market. No one knows what will happen in the next minute. People lose millions in seconds.

To control your emotions at that time is a hard task. But to become a mature trader, you must have the capability to see your pockets running out of money. With a relaxed mind, you can set a plan B and C to get things in the right direction.

12- 360 Degree View

Experienced traders always dive deep into learning more about stocks every day. This is the reason because of which you gain more and more experience. Whether you are buying or selling stocks shares, you always be completely aware of what you are doing.

You must be clear about what its outcomes will be. There must be some strategies for the sudden uncertainty to keep you stable in the market.

13- Automate stocks

Automating your stocks is a key activity to gain more experience in the stock market. It also helps to build your security and play on the safe side. If you are not willing to do it manually, then Robo-Advisors are always there to assist you. When you have a habit of regular investments, then you also avoid timing the market strategy.

14- Say no to leverage

Leverage simply refers to start investing in stocks by borrowing money. There are many ways to borrow money. For example, you can also borrow from brokerage firms. Some people who are new to the stock market use this method to start their stock market journey. There are bright chances of their failure because of high risks are involved. This strategy can do work for you when you have gained much experience in stocks.

15- Choose one sector

Investing in one sector can be a better approach. Professional traders always invest in one sector. There are many advantages to investing in one sector. If your focus is on one industry, you will learn more in a short time. You will also start getting familiar with the fluctuations in the industry.

16- Risk vs. Return

Simply, more risky investments always have chances of big profits. On the other hand, less risky investments have small profit margins. So, you have to be clear with your game plan that how much return; you are willing to have. People always make foolish mistakes and goes for high-profit margins and lose their money. So instead of regretting at that time, invest in between high and low-risk investments.

17- Buy low sell higher

This is the most well-known method which almost all the traders apply. But some people get wrong with this strategy, and instead of making a profit, they end up with the loss. One of the most important factors to consider while buying low price stocks is to calculate their standard deviation.

If the stocks in which you are interested in buying to have a 15% standard deviation, you are good to go. It will be a better strategy if your stock standard deviation falls below then 15% in a short period. There are bright chances of that specific stock that now it will go up.

Final Word

Many people believe that stocks are a scam, but if you set up things in the right direction, then these stocks can make you more profit than any other business in the world. All you need is not to focus on investing your money in the stock market, but you need to invest your time to learn the stock market. No one can ever predict with 100% surety about the stocks.

But by gaining more experience, you can understand the behavior of stocks and learn about the fluctuations. Before going for the live trade, considers all the above-mentioned tips and tricks for investing in the stock market to make your journey in stocks successful.

CONCLUSION

Thank you for downloading my book on stock market investment. It is a self-help book for newbies who want to start as investors and make money. Filled with top rules, regulations, important terms, and strategies that one should know before jumping into the investment game, the book encompasses all the beneficial information needed for new investors.

Here is one question for you, may I ask? What did you learn from this book? Can you recall?

Here is what I tell everyone to remember while investing in the stock exchange:

"Rule number one: Don't lose money. Rule number two: Don't forget rule number one."

Warren Buffett

How can you make this sure? Follow the set of advice, suggestions, and guidelines given in this book. Hope you found it helpful and worthy to keep. Please do not forget to give us your feedback so we can improve further.

Thank you, Happy Investing!

www.ingramcontent.com/pod-product-compliance
Lightning Source LLC
Chambersburg PA
CBHW070634220526
45466CB00001B/173